A Medieval Manor House Rediscovered
Excavations at Longforth Farm, Wellington, Somerset

Simon Flaherty, Phil Andrews and Matt Leivers

A Medieval Manor House Rediscovered

Excavations at Longforth Farm, Wellington, Somerset

Simon Flaherty, Phil Andrews and Matt Leivers

with contributions by Bob Davis, L. Higbee, Laura Joyner,
Lorraine Mepham, Mary Siraut and Sarah F. Wyles

Illustrations by
Karen Nichols and S. E. James

Wessex Archaeology Occasional Paper
2016

Published 2016 by Wessex Archaeology Ltd
Portway House, Old Sarum Park, Salisbury, SP4 6EB
www.wessexarch.co.uk

Copyright © 2016 Wessex Archaeology Ltd
All rights reserved

British Library Cataloguing in Publication Data
A catalogue record for this book is available from the British Library

ISBN 978-1-874350-85-9

Designed and typeset by Kenneth Lymer
Cover design by Karen Nichols
Copy-edited by Philippa Bradley
Printed by Latimer Trend & Company, Plymouth

Front cover
Visualisation of manor house complex, from north-east

Back cover
Top: Excavation of manor house complex in progress, view from south
Middle: Fragment of 'Richard and Saladin' floor tile
Bottom: Open day site tour

Wessex Archaeology Ltd is a company limited by guarantee registered in England, company number 1712772. It is also a Charity registered in England and Wales number 287786, and in Scotland, Scottish Charity number SC042630. Our registered office is at Portway House, Old Sarum Park, Salisbury, Wiltshire, SP4 6EB.

Contents

List of Figures vi
List of Plates vi
List of Tables vii
Acknowledgements viii
Abstract viii

Chapter 1: Introduction
The site 1
Archaeological background 2
Previous investigations 3
Outreach at Longforth Farm, *by Laura Joyner* 3

Chapter 2: Historical Evidence
by Mary Siraut
The site 4
The manor of Wellington 4
The manor house 4
The Thomas family and Drakes Place 6
Culverhayes and neighbouring fields 7
Longforth Farm 7

Chapter 3: The Excavations
Chronology and phasing 9
Period 1: Prehistoric to Romano-British 9
    Earlier prehistoric finds 9
    Bronze Age landscape organisation 9
    Iron Age and Romano-British material 12
Period 2: Medieval 13
    Early features 13
    The building complex 13
    Drainage 22
    Associated enclosures 24
    Palaeochannel 10112 27
    Other ditches and gullies 27
Period 3: Later medieval/post-medieval 28
    Area B 28
    Areas C and D 29

Chapter 4: Building Materials
Building stone, *by Bob Davis* 30
    Foundations 30
    Walling 30
Roofing slate, *by Lorraine Mepham* 30
Ceramic building material,
    by Lorraine Mepham 32
    Ridge tiles 32
    Floor tiles 34
    Floor/hearth tiles 36

Chapter 5: Finds
Pottery, *by Lorraine Mepham* 37
    Prehistoric and Romano-British 37
    Medieval 38
    Post-medieval 41
    Discussion 41
Worked and burnt flint, *by Matt Leivers* 43
Other finds, *by Lorraine Mepham* 43

Chapter 6: Environment and Economy
Animal bone, *by L. Higbee* 44
    Preservation 44
    Medieval material 44
Marine shell, *by Sarah F. Wyles* 44
Charred plant remains, *by Sarah F. Wyles* 44
    Methods 44
    Results 45
    Discussion 48

Chapter 7: Discussion
Prehistoric and Romano-British 49
Medieval and later 49
Conclusion 56

Bibliography 58

List of Figures

Chapter 1
Figure 1.1　Site location plan

Chapter 2
Figure 2.1　Excavation areas superimposed on 1st edition OS map, with field names and other features taken from 1839 tithe map

Chapter 3
Figure 3.1　Prehistoric features in Area B
Figure 3.2　Prehistoric features in Area A
Figure 3.3　Prehistoric features in Areas C and D
Figure 3.4　Medieval features in Area B
Figure 3.5　Reconstructed layout of medieval manor house
Figure 3.6　Visualisation of north elevation of manor house
Figure 3.7　Plan of garderobe
Figure 3.8　Visualisation of south elevation of hall, solar and entrance from courtyard
Figure 3.9　Visualisation of service range, detached kitchen and east end of ancillary building
Figure 3.10　Plan of ancillary building
Figure 3.11　Plan of medieval features to east of manor house
Figure 3.12　Plan of post-medieval features in area of manor house
Figure 3.13　Plan of post-medieval features in Areas C and D

Chapter 4
Figure 4.1　Slate roof-tiles (numbers 1–9)
Figure 4.2　Ceramic ridge tiles (numbers 1–5)
Figure 4.3　Ceramic floor tiles (number 1–8)

Chapter 5
Figure 5.1　Prehistoric pottery (numbers 1–3)
Figure 5.2　Medieval pottery (numbers 1–9)

Chapter 7
Figure 7.1　Visualisation of north elevation of manor house, service range, detached kitchen and east end of ancillary building, from north-east
Figure 7.2　Visualisation of interior of hall at first floor level
Figure 7.3　Visualisation of courtyard and surrounding buildings, from south-west
Figure 7.4　Ecclesiastical estates in Somerset (after Aston 1988)

List of Plates

Chapter 1
Plate 1.1　Overview of excavations in progress, with Nynehead Park in distance, from south-east
Plate 1.2　Visitors and finds (© Rob Perrett Photography)
Plate 1.3　Site open day (© Rob Perrett Photography)

Chapter 3
Plate 3.1　Overview of excavations in progress, with hall area in centre, from north-east
Plate 3.2　Terminal Upper Palaeolithic blade
Plate 3.3　Overview of excavations in progress, with forecourt in foreground, solar area in centre, hall area to left, from north
Plate 3.4　Wall foundation 10077 – west wall of hall, from north-east
Plate 3.5　Hall buttress 729, from north
Plate 3.6　Hall buttresses a) 1085, from south; b) 791, from east
Plate 3.7　Base of garderobe 10048, from south
Plate 3.8　Room 8 in foreground, with solar area (left) and hall area (right) behind, from south
Plate 3.9　Detached kitchen (Room 9) – wall 10106, with Room 6 in background, and walls 1403 and 10103 to right, from south-east
Plate 3.10　Overview of excavations in progress, with ancillary building 10 in foreground, from south-east
Plate 3.11　Drain 10071 within ancillary building/Room 10; south wall 10040

Plate 3.12	(note shallower wall foundations to right), from north
Plate 3.12	Drain 10071 in ancillary building/Room 10; external exit through north wall 1038 into courtyard (note offset of wall 695 to right), from north
Plate 3.13	Drain 10071 in ancillary building/Room 10; external opening through south wall 10040, from south
Plate 3.14	Drain 10044 around exterior of Room 8, from south-west
Plate 3.15	Base of garderobe 10048, from south-east
Plate 3.16	Detail of base of garderobe 10048, from south
Plate 3.17	Forecourt, south-west corner, with wall 769 to right and drain 10117 from garderobe to left, from north-west
Plate 3.18	Overview of excavations in progress, with medieval pit complex to right and palaeochannel 10112 to left, with manor house in background, from south-east

Chapter 5
Plate 5.1   Costrel (fabric Q409) from ditch 10095

Chapter 7
Plate 7.1   Overview of excavations in progress, with ancillary building in foreground, detached kitchen (centre right), and solar (left), hall (centre) and service range (right) beyond, from south-east
Plate 7.2   Crested, glazed ridge tiles
Plate 7.3   Decorated floor tiles

List of Tables

Chapter 2
Table 2.1   Holdings of William Procter Thomas, gentleman in 1766, according to land tax assessment (SHC, Q/RE1 24/5)

Chapter 4
Table 4.1   Ceramic building material by type
Table 4.2   Decorated floor tile designs (design numbers follow Lowe 2003; Wells designs from Rodwell 2001)

Chapter 5
Table 5.1   Medieval and post-medieval pottery fabric totals
Table 5.2   Other finds by material type

Chapter 6
Table 6.1   Charred plant remains from medieval features

Acknowledgements

Wessex Archaeology is very grateful to Bloor Homes Ltd, and especially Christopher Davis, for commissioning and funding the project. Steven Membery and Tanya James of Somerset County Council (now South West Heritage Trust) are also thanked for their help and advice, particularly during the course of the fieldwork.

The project was managed on behalf of Wessex Archaeology by Caroline Budd and the post-excavation programme was managed by Matt Leivers. The excavations were directed by Simon Flaherty and John Powell, with the assistance of Darryl Freer and Ray Kennedy. The fieldwork was undertaken by a team of more than 30 people, the following of whom were on site for the majority of the excavation: Jeremy Austin, Mark Bagwell, Phil Breach, David Browne, Charlotte Burton, Ralph Collard, Martyn Cooper, Samuel Fairhead, Margaret Feryok, Thomas Firth, Michael Fleming, Fiona Gamble, Ed Grenier, Mark Hackney, Jane Harris, Adam Howard, Amy McCabe, Jamie McCarthy, Dave Murdie, Tina Tapply, Alan Whittaker and Dane Wright. Overhead images were provided by Aerial-Cam, and we would like to thank Adam Stanford.

The programme of community engagement activities was organised and run by Laura Joyner, with assistance from Marc Cox of Somerset County Council (now South West Heritage Trust). This programme was supported and entirely funded by Bloor Homes, facilitated in particular by Michele Rose. Rob Perrett (of Rob Perrett Photography) is thanked for photography during the open day.

The environmental samples were processed by Tony Scothern and Eleanor Stevens, and the peat sample from the palaeochannel was examined by Nicki Mulhall. We are particularly grateful to Mary Siraut for undertaking the documentary research, using the facilities available at the Somerset Heritage Centre, Taunton. Bob Davis discussed various aspects of the medieval building remains, and Karen Nichols used the results of these discussions in converting the two-dimensional site plan into a three-dimensional visualisation. The other plans have been drawn by Karen Nichols and the finds illustrated by Elizabeth James. This report was edited by Philippa Bradley.

Finally, we would like to acknowledge the unprecedented interest and support provided by the people of Wellington and the surrounding area, which greatly raised the public profile of the important discoveries made at Longforth Farm in 2013.

The project archive for the excavations will be deposited with Somerset County Museum, Taunton, under the accession code TTNCM 90/2012

Abstract

Excavations in advance of housing development at Longforth Farm, Wellington, Somerset, revealed limited evidence for late prehistoric settlement, but the principal discovery was the remains of a previously unknown high status medieval building complex. This is thought to have been a manor house and though heavily robbed, key elements identified include a hall, solar with garderobe and service wing. A forecourt lay to the north and a courtyard with at least one ancillary building and a possible detached kitchen to the south. To the east was a complex of enclosures and pits and beyond this a fishpond.

There was a restricted range and number of medieval finds, but together these suggest that occupation spanned the late 12th/early 13th century to the late 14th/early 15th century. There was a notable group of medieval floor tiles and roof furniture, but documentary research has failed to identify the owners and any records relating specifically to this important building. One possibility is that it belonged to the Bishops of Bath and Wells, and was perhaps abandoned around the end of the 14th century when they may have moved their court to within the nearby and then relatively new market town of Wellington.

Chapter 1
Introduction

Wessex Archaeology was commissioned by Bloor Homes Ltd to undertake excavations at Longforth Farm, Wellington, Somerset (NGR 311403 122148), in advance of proposed large-scale housing development (Fig.1.1).

The excavations, carried out in 2012 and 2013, represented an element within a staged programme of archaeological work that began in 2010. The earlier elements, outlined in greater detail below, comprised geophysical survey (Bournemouth University 2010), desk-based assessment (Terence O'Rourke 2011) and evaluation trenching (Cotswold Archaeology 2011a). These were used to produce a mitigation strategy, set out in a Written Scheme of Investigation (WSI) (Cotswold Archaeology 2011b), which formed part of an Environmental Impact Statement for the proposed development.

The Site

The development area as a whole is approximately 50 ha in extent and comprised agricultural land, principally pasture, with some arable. It is located on the north-eastern edge of Wellington and is bounded to the north by the London to Penzance railway line, to the east by Nynehead Road, to the south by Taunton Road and the town of Wellington, and to the west by factories (Fig.1.1). The site lies at approximately 58 m above Ordnance Datum (OD) in the east, rising to 68 m OD in the centre, before sloping down to 52 m OD in the west.

The solid geology of the site predominantly comprises Triassic sandstone of the Otter Formation, overlain in the north-western part by clay, sand and gravel. The eastern part comprises Sidmouth

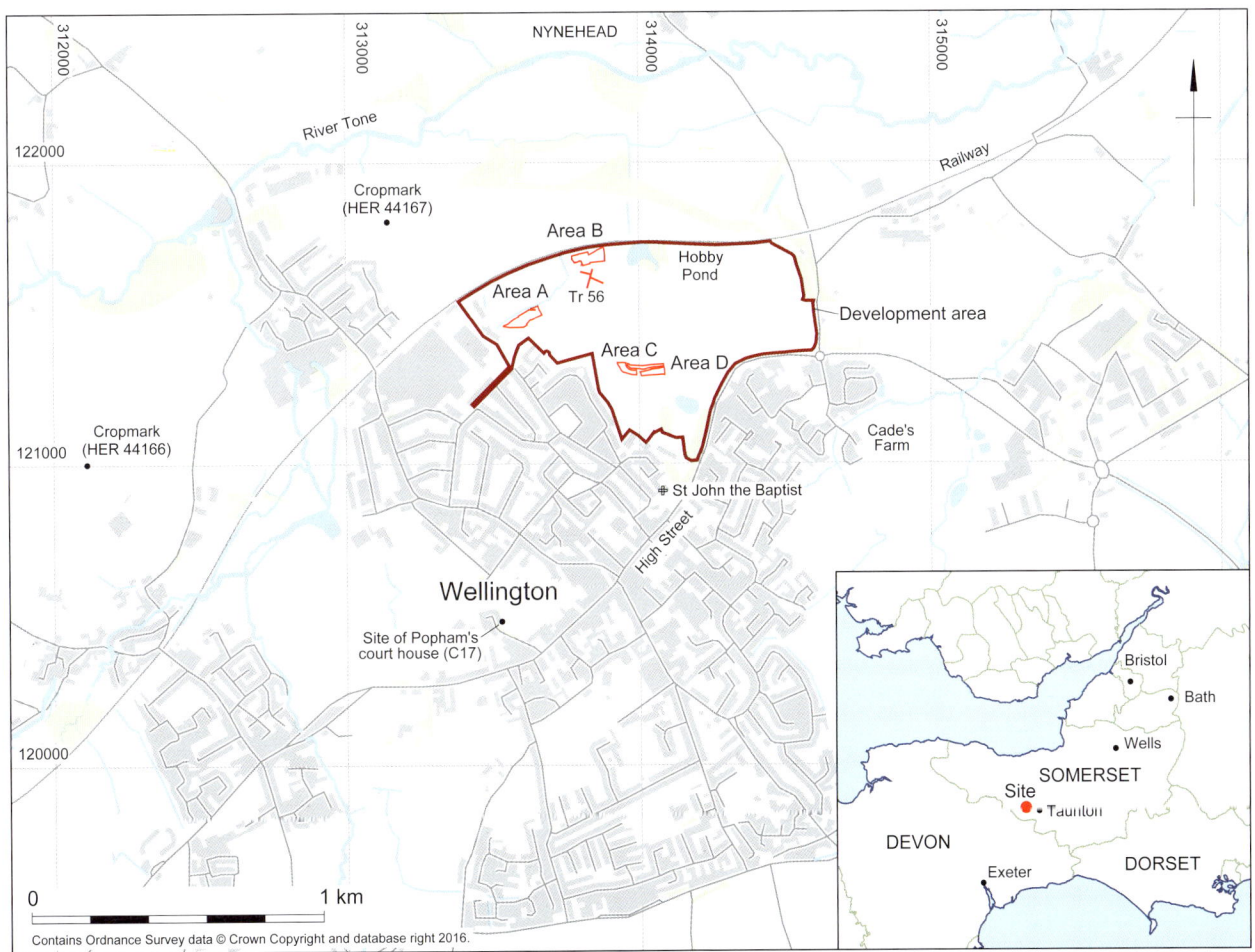

Figure 1.1 Site location plan

Plate 1.1 Overview of excavations in progress, with Nynehead Park in distance, from south-east

Mudstone of the Triassic period (British Geological Survey 2013).

Archaeological Background

The earlier prehistoric period is sparsely represented within the area surrounding the site. Surface finds mainly comprise a small number of unstratified worked flint or stone tools, most attributable to the Neolithic or Bronze Age, with a single Bronze Age copper alloy axe recovered approximately 300 m to the south-west (Gathercole 2003, 6). No pre-Roman features were found during fairly extensive evaluations at Cade's Farm immediately to the south-east, and there was only a single sherd of Iron Age pottery (Oxford Archaeological Unit (OAU) 1997; Cotswold Archaeology 2005). Aerial photographs show cropmarks of a rectangular, double-ditched enclosure (HER 44167; Gathercole 2003) of possible prehistoric date a short distance to the north-west, and those of a trapezoidal enclosure further to the west (HER 44166; Gathercole 2003) (Fig. 1.1).

The evaluations at Cade's Farm identified only limited evidence for Romano-British settlement activity, in the form of a pair of ditches, with a unurned cremation burial inserted into the top of one, and a small pottery assemblage, amongst which was a group of sherds which suggested production nearby (OAU 1997; Cotswold Archaeology 2005). Evidence of Roman activity is also recorded approximately 1 km north of the site, just south of Nynehead (Terence O'Rourke 2011), and 2 km to the south a farmstead was investigated in advance of construction of the M5 (Gathercole 2003, 7).

Although first recorded in a royal land grant of AD 904, it is unclear what the settlement at Wellington consisted of at that time. However, by the *Domesday* Survey of 1086 it appears to have been relatively well populated, and a watching brief at St John the Baptist's Church (Fig.1.1) suggested that the current church occupies the site of a Norman predecessor (Croft 1987). The settlement was given town status in a charter of 1215 which, as well as Wellington, also included Axbridge and Chard. The medieval street plan of a long central road that was wider in the centre of the town to accommodate the market place, with a regularly spaced arrangement of properties and a church at the (east) end, is typical of towns laid out in the 12th and 13th centuries (Gathercole 2003). By 1345 the borough, under the auspices of the Bishops of Bath and Wells, had a number of denoted burgesses and was the focus of several markets and fairs, as well as being a minor centre of cloth production.

Previous Investigations

Initially, Bournemouth University undertook a geophysical survey of approximately 31 ha of the site (Bournemouth University 2010). The survey identified various linear, curvilinear and discrete anomalies across most of the fields, some of which appeared to be evidence of past human activity. Due to their inconclusive nature many of the anomalies could not be confidently interpreted; there was sufficient evidence, however, to suggest that several possible enclosures were present. Other anomalies were thought likely to represent drainage features associated with modern agricultural practices, and some represented disturbance associated with the construction of the 19th-century railway line along the northern boundary of the northern fields.

Subsequent archaeological evaluation, undertaken by Cotswold Archaeology in early 2011, identified a probable trackway of potentially Bronze Age date and three pits containing 12th- to 14th-century pottery (Cotswold Archaeology 2011a). There were also a number of ditches relating to land division and water management, several corresponding to the alignment of the existing field system, elements of which were thought likely to date to the post-medieval or possibly medieval periods.

Outreach at Longforth Farm
by Laura Joyner

Plate 1.2 Visitors and finds (© Rob Perrett Photography)

Plate 1.3 Site open day (© Rob Perrett Photography)

The discovery and recognition of the remains of what transpired to be a hitherto unknown medieval manor house (Pl. 1.1) generated an exceptional level of local interest. In response to this a series of events was organised over a single week in early July 2013, comprising a media day, school workshops, local history society tours and a community open day. This involved Wessex Archaeology and the site developers, Bloor Homes, as well as Somerset County Council, and proved to be extremely popular.

The media day was well attended by members of the local and regional press, including the *Wellington Weekly News* and the *Somerset County Gazette*, and *Current Archaeology*. Television crews from regional news teams ITV *Somerset* and BBC *Points West* were also present. Media interest in the site built throughout the programme of events and afterwards, with several publications and a local radio station reporting on the success of the community open day.

On-site school workshops took place over three days and over 250 children from four local schools took part. The workshops featured a tour of the archaeological site and the opportunity to design medieval floor tiles using clay. Students were able to view the artefacts from the excavation and encouraged to ask questions and engage with the archaeology (Pl. 1.2).

The local historical society tours proved popular and were fully booked, with over 80 members of local historical groups visiting.

The week of events culminated in a community open day which offered local residents the opportunity to be shown round the site and discover more about Wellington's heritage. Over 1400 people came to this free event, which included several children's activities, an unprecedented number that reflected the considerable local interest in the site (Pl. 1.3).

Following the open day, displays about the archaeological discoveries were mounted at Wellington Museum and in the show-home of the new development. Subsequently, talks and lectures on the site have been given at various local, regional and national events.

Chapter 2
Historical Evidence

by Mary Siraut

Unfortunately there are few medieval records for Wellington so it is impossible to give a coherent history of the town's early development. However, using 19th-century maps and deeds and other materials from the late 16th century it is possible to give a picture of the landownership and farmsteads in the area.

The Site

The site lies on the northern edge of a field called Great Moor, immediately to the south of a field called Culverhayes (Fig. 2.1). The latter belonged to the Pophams' Wellington Landside manor until they sold it in 1749 to William Procter Thomas of Drakes Place, whose family had been tenants for over a century. The name signifies there was a dovecot in the field, which would suggest a house or farmstead was nearby but no record of it has been found.

Culverhayes and Great Moor lie north of the town on low and probably damp land south of the River Tone in an area disrupted by the construction of the canal and later the railway. A large pond now known as Hobby Pond, a fish pond in 1839, lies to the east and presumably drained into the substantial tributary of the Tone, formerly the course of the river, which has been diverted in Nynehead Park. Approximately 50 m to the west along the hedge line there was formerly a road to Nynehead, abandoned in the early 19th century but still marked as a footpath on the 1st edition of the 6" OS map and partly surviving today.

The nearest farmstead is now Longforth Farm but in the 18th century there were several others around the site. The pattern of lanes and paths in the area has also been changed partly because of building development. Housing and a factory now cover many of the fields around Longforth Farm.

The Manor of Wellington

Wellington manor, with Buckland, belonged to the Bishops of Bath and Wells in the Middle Ages. They gave the church and its property with land in West Buckland before 1234 to the Provost of Wells Cathedral. That estate later passed to the Dean and formed the Dean of Wells' manor of Wellington and Buckland, which was transferred in the 1840s to the Ecclesiastical Commissioners. Their property was around the church and in West Buckland.

The Wellington family had an estate in the Middle Ages, probably Northam manor about which little is known but whose lands appear to have been in a different part of the parish.

The main manor of Wellington was divided into Wellington Manor and the Borough Manor by 1302, following the creation of the town. Both belonged to the bishops until they were forced to sell to the Duke of Somerset in 1548. In 1550 the duke sold the Borough back to the bishop retaining the other manor that became known as Wellington Landside, and sometimes Landslide! After Somerset's execution (22 January 1552) for felony Wellington Landside passed to the Crown which bought back the Borough Manor and gave both to the Duke of Northumberland in 1553 shortly before he was executed and once again both manors were held by the Crown. In 1624 James I sold them to trustees for Sir Francis Popham.

The Popham family retained the manors until the mid-18th century when they were sold separately. They were reunited after 1813 in the ownership of the Duke of Wellington until the Borough was sold to local trustees in 1883.

Few manorial records survive except for some medieval court rolls, printed in 1910 (Humphreys 1910).

The Manor House

The whereabouts of the bishops' court is unknown, but the assembled evidence presented here is used to suggest that the building remains uncovered at Longforth Farm represent the bishops' earliest medieval manor house in Wellington. Manor houses are usually near the church but Wellington bears the hallmarks of a planned settlement and its earlier layout is unclear. The Pophams chose to build their new Court House within the town possibly on or near the site of a Borough court house, said to have been a 15th-century building; the new Court House was destroyed in 1645 during the Civil War.

The bishops rarely visited Wellington and then only for a day on their way to or from Wiveliscombe, which was the preferred West Somerset home of 14th-century bishops like Ralph of Shrewsbury.

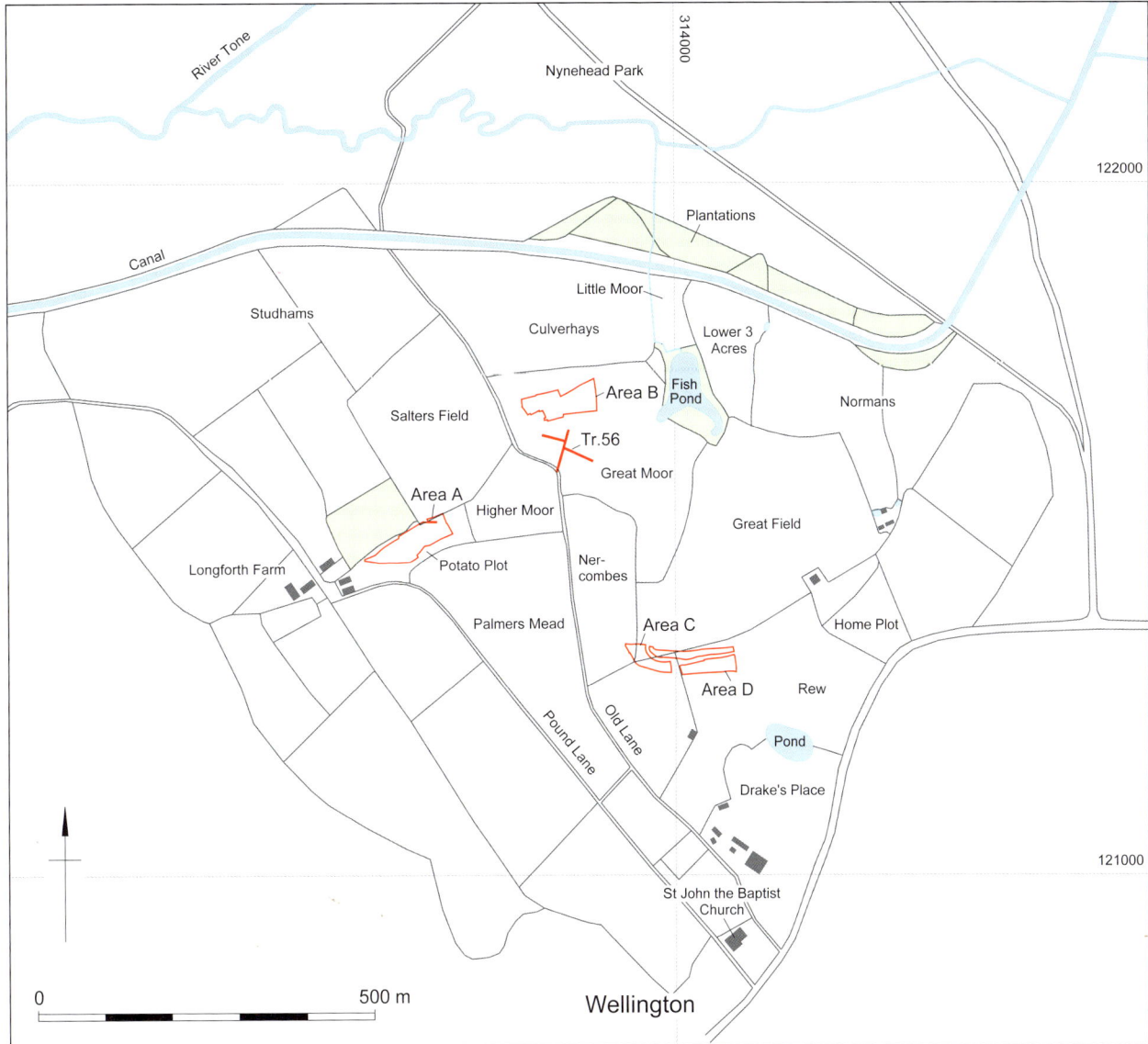

Figure 2.1 Excavation areas superimposed on 1st edition OS map, with field names and other features taken from 1839 tithe map

Bishops do not seem to have visited in the 15th century and the bishops' manor house may have been abandoned at an early date (Register of Bishop Drokensford, Somerset Record Society 9–10; Register of Bishop Ralph of Shrewsbury, Somerset Record Society 1).

The only documentary references come from the court rolls:

1343 Houses in the Court need thatching, which was the reeve's responsibility;
1353 Houses in the Court need repair, the reeve's responsibility;
1373 Reference to the cherry trees in the lord's garden, damaged and fruit stolen;
1382 A man was falsely accused of taking chalk from the lord's Court;
1383 Two servants of John Trenchard were accused of taking lime from the lord's cellar under the lord's hall to the house of John Fenne. Both brought witnesses to prove they were not guilty (Humphreys 1910).

There are no other references to the lord's court or buildings.

Sir John de Molton, who normally appears to have lived in the Chard area, was licensed to have services for his household in his chapel at Wellington in 1343. It is just possible he was the tenant of the bishop's manor house but perhaps more likely of Northam or elsewhere (Register of Bishop Drokensford, Somerset Record Society 1). He was still in Wellington in 1344 (Cornwall RO, AR/1/1 101).

Table 2.1 Holdings of William Procter Thomas, gentleman in 1766, according to land tax assessment (SHC, Q/RE1 24/5)

Wellington: Westford tithing	
Owns:	
Homething and Cood Close	£3 7s 10d
Normans	£3 1s 8d
Long Causey Houses (houses dropped by 1800s)	12s 2d
Salters	£1 17s
Drakes and Old Place	£4 6s 4d
Longforth – abated for paying towards almshouses	£2 6s 3d
Sheepland	12s 4d
Churchground	£1 17s
Drakesland (later Dukesland)	£2 9s 4d
Woolcotts (formerly called Henry Woolcotts (Walcott))	£1 4s 8d
Nurtons Culverhayes (later Nurtons and Culverhayes)	18s 6d

He also owned other property elsewhere in Wellington.

The family normally occupied Drakes and Old Place, with the rest let off mostly to the Ferrant family, gentleman farmers of Longforth Farm.

The Thomas family were still holding properties until 1830s – last land tax assessment.

The Thomas Family and Drakes Place

The first member of the Thomas family associated with Westford tithing in Wellington was John Thomas who had Old Place.

On 1 May 1595 he leased from Richard Best of Wellington a house with an orchard on the south and west, Poole Close (5 acres north of the house) and Wester Close (4.5 acres west of Poole Close), Moore Mead adjoining Poole Close (2 acres) and More Platt (1 acre) in Washford [sic] tithing in Wellington formerly occupied by John Hancock alias Thomas deceased, for the lives of himself and his wife Alice. The deed is endorsed in a later hand 'lease of Old Place' and in 1611 George Best sold the property with fields called Gladney and Fries Ground to John Thomas. Unfortunately the fields in this area had been amalgamated and renamed by the 19th century but the closes named may have made up the later Great Field (Fig. 2.1).

John Thomas died c. 1632 leaving a wife Alice and son Roger. Roger Thomas and his son Roger both died in 1671, the latter leaving a widow Jane died c. 1726 and a son John died c. 1735. John married Honor, co-heiress of John Procter of West Monkton, who brought land and wealth to the Thomas family. They had six children but the elder son John died 1748 unmarried and his brother William Procter Thomas succeeded. William bought out the interests of his three surviving sisters and finished the building of Drakes Place. It was he who bought Culverhayes and other lands of which his family had been tenants from Edward Popham in 1749. William married Frances Gunston of Bishops Hull and served as steward of Wellington manor. He died before 1803 and was succeeded by his son the Revd William Procter Thomas, who in April 1811 married Arabella Maria Bayley of Sampford Arundel by whom he had two daughters but divorced her in 1818 for her adultery with Robert Tyser of Tiverton.

A tenement called Drakes, which may be the predecessor of the Thomas family's property of the same name, was held by the Bicknell family in 1613 and covered 10 acres. The later Drakes Place grounds were approximately 13 acres so it is possible that this land was the site of Drakes Place in the mid-18th century (Fig. 2.1). Any earlier house on the property may have been on the street by the church to which the later grounds extend.

Drakes Place appears to have been built in the early 18th century to replace Old Place by John Thomas and his brother William Procter Thomas who spent £1500 finishing it after John's death on 28 September 1748. In 1748–9 he completed the parlour chamber and the furnishing of the parlour and drawing room; also he added a linhay and repaired Longforth and the Old House barn. The west part of the mansion including kitchen and pantries were completed in 1753–4 followed by the walled garden and open stables. He pulled down Old Place and planted the site as Place Orchard, possibly Old Orchard (1760 on tithe). The farm buildings, described as Old Farm on the 1st edition OS 1" map, were standing in 1822 but had gone by 1839 (SHC, DD/DP 35/3, 63/3, 64/3, 73/2, 93/8-9; Greenwoods map of Somerset 1822; SHC, Wellington tithe award 1839).

Culverhayes and Neighbouring Fields

Although occupied by the Thomas family since 1728 or earlier Culverhayes was only bought by William Procter Thomas in 1749 from Edward Popham. It was therefore part of Wellington Landside manor and formerly part of Bishop's manor of Wellington. William Procter Thomas also bought from Popham Northams alias Salters, Homething and Code Close with cottage property and small plots that he later sold off (Table 2.1). The family also bought Normans, east of Culverhayes (Fig. 2.1), which had an old messuage and barn in the 1740s, presumably on the site of the linhays on the tithe map north-west of the Old Farm site. Clearly there were more farmsteads in this part of Wellington in the mid-18th century than there were by the 1839 tithe commutation.

The tithe award shows that the Thomas family had lost some land. The Sanfords of Nynehead had bought land north of the canal, now cut off from rest of Thomas family's Wellington lands.

The Thomas family let out their farmland in the mid-19th century and by 1842, when many of their fields including Culverhayes lost land to the Bristol and Exeter railway, some fields including Great Moor south of Culverhayes were let with Longforth Farm and the rest including Culverhayes were let as Old House Farm for which a farmstead was built on the site of Norman's linhays after 1842. It is shown on the 1st edition OS 6" map but has since been demolished (SHC, DD/DP 85/5).

Longforth Farm

Longforth Farm (Fig. 2.1) was let to members of the Walcott and Shorland families in the 17th century (History of the Walcott Family; SHC, DD/SF 2/57/19) and in the 18th century was often known as Shorlands. In the 19th century it was farmed by the Ferrant or Farrant family with the almshouse charity lands (SHC, DD/DP 42/5; DD/SF 2/42/71; A/DAE 1/15).

Chapter 3
The Excavations

In light of the results of the evaluation and geophysical survey (see Chapter 1), a programme of archaeological mitigation was developed for the site. A project design was written by Cotswold Archaeology (2011b) and this document along with later revisions formed the basis for the excavation strategy. Four areas of the proposed 50 ha development were targeted for excavation, together totalling almost 1.5 ha (see Fig. 1.1).

Area A (5480 m²) was located towards the west side of the site and was targeted on evaluation trenches 12 and 13. A possible hollow-way from which Bronze Age pottery was recovered and two undated ditches had been identified in trench 13, and two broadly parallel ditches that contained medieval pottery were found in trench 12.

Area B (initially 2150 m²) lay towards the north edge of the site, south of the existing railway line. The area was targeted on three medieval pits and several ditches revealed within evaluation trench 7 and on an undated ditch in trench 8, the latter shown on Ordnance Survey maps and appearing in the geophysical survey results. Stripping revealed an enclosure system on the eastern side of the site and the remains of a medieval building complex on the west. This area was further extended to the west to expose the full extent of the complex and as far north as the railway line (an overall area of 3690 m²). The building complex had been heavily robbed and comprised robber trenches, a number of *in situ* footings and, in a few places, more substantial masonry remains (Pl. 3.1).

Following the discovery of the medieval building complex a cross-shaped evaluation trench (tr. 56) was excavated across a possible building platform located approximately 20 m to the south of Area B. The north-east to south-west element of the trench was 63.5 m long, whilst the two south-east to north-west elements had a total length of 80 m. The trench revealed a small number of similarly-aligned ditches but no further building remains.

Plate 3.1 Overview of excavations in progress, with hall area in centre, from north-east

Area C (3565 m²) was targeted on an undated curvilinear ditch and postholes identified within evaluation trench 28. Area D (2980 m²) was located directly to the east of Area C and separated from it by a modern field boundary. Area D was targeted on three undated ditches identified within evaluation trench 34.

Chronology and Phasing

The site stratigraphy, along with an initial assessment of the relatively small assemblage of artefactual remains, was used to establish a provisional dated sequence within which most excavated contexts could be placed (Wessex Archaeology 2014). A more detailed examination of the records and the finds, especially the pottery, later allowed the sequence to be further refined and more securely dated, but close dating has generally proved difficult for all periods.

Three periods of activity have been identified. The following sections provide details of the excavated sequence by period and phase, where appropriate. The medieval building materials are described in Chapter 4, and the artefacts discussed by material type and period in Chapter 5, with catalogues in the archive. The environmental data are described within Chapter 6 and the results of the documentary research are set out in Chapter 2, above.

Prehistoric (Period 1) deposits contained a small number of pieces of diagnostic worked flint, however most of this material occurred residually in later contexts. The little dating evidence that there is suggests there were generally low levels of activity from the Palaeolithic through to the Iron Age. The only prehistoric features that have been identified with any confidence probably belong to the Middle Bronze Age and the Late Bronze Age–Early Iron Age respectively, and there were no Romano-British remains other than a few sherds of pottery.

Medieval activity (Period 2) appears to have spanned the late 12th or early 13th century through to the late 14th or early 15th century. The later medieval and post-medieval phase (Period 3) was largely identified on the basis of stratigraphy, particularly in Area B where the features cut through the remains of the earlier medieval building complex.

Period 1: Prehistoric to Romano-British

Earlier Prehistoric Finds

Indications of earlier prehistoric activity on the site were limited, consisting only of redeposited lithics, most from Area A. The earliest of these is a large Terminal Upper Palaeolithic blade made from

Plate 3.2 Terminal Upper Palaeolithic blade

Greensand chert (Pl. 3.2), recovered from the interface of the natural and the subsoil towards the eastern end of the area. The piece is in very good condition and appears to belong to a Long Blade tradition, dating to around 9500–8500 BC. No other material of this date was present.

Several flint blades, broken blades and blade and bladelet cores of Mesolithic date were found in the topsoil, particularly in the vicinity of Area A, and also in linear hollow 10002, in part perhaps an overflow channel. This feature also contained a single Neolithic end scraper and a small number of sherds of Bronze Age pottery, indicating that the Mesolithic lithics were residual. In addition, the distal portion of a lateral truncation came from ditch 10009 and a serrated blade from ditch 10003, both these Mesolithic finds also from Area A.

Other than the material in Area A, earlier prehistoric material was limited to a single Mesolithic flint blade from tree-throw hole 264 in Area D.

Bronze Age Landscape Organisation

Middle Bronze Age

The earliest features on the site that could be dated with any confidence were located in Area B (Fig. 3.1). At the western end of this area was a SSW to NNE aligned gully (10092), adjacent to the eastern edge of palaeochannel 10113. The gully was very shallow and continued for 5 m before terminating. It contained a

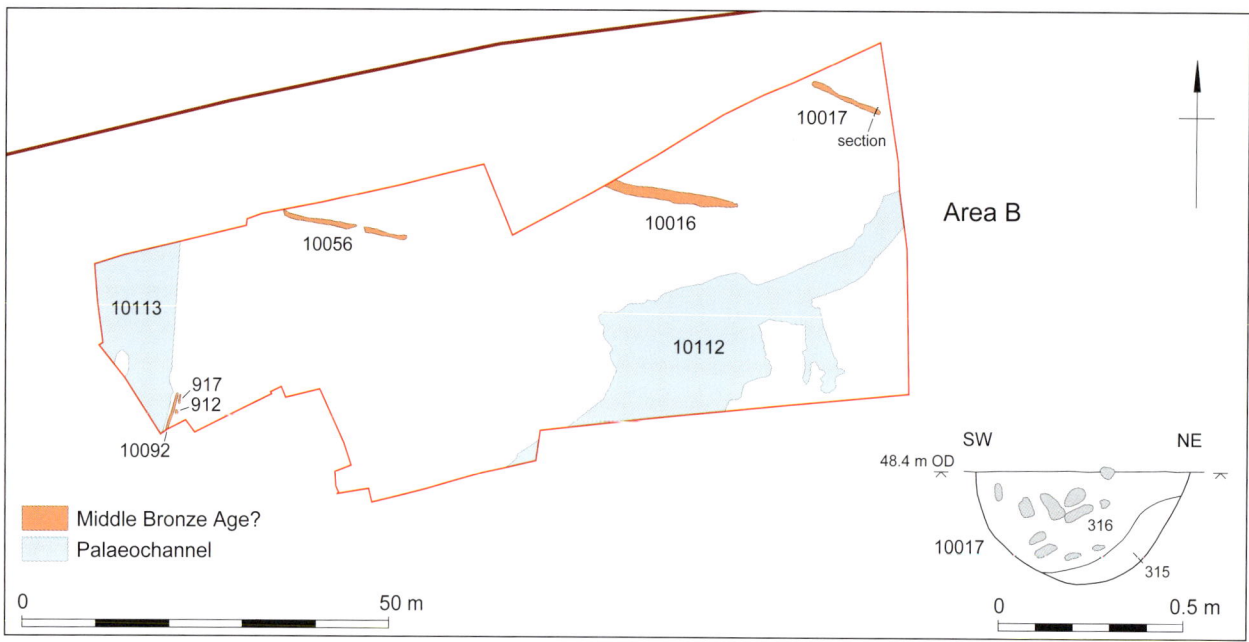

Figure 3.1 Prehistoric features in Area B

single flint scraper of Bronze Age date. A further two features were located next to the gully: a possible pit (912) and the partial remnants of a second gully (917) that was parallel to 10092. Although no dating evidence was found in either, their close proximity to gully 10092 and the fact they lay 0.65 m deeper than the medieval archaeology in this area suggests that all were of a similar date.

Palaeochannel 10113, probably a branch of palaeochannel 10112 (see below), was only partially revealed at the western end of the area, where it was 0.3 m deep and at least 10 m wide. It ran in a north-east to south-west direction and was cut by medieval features, but no finds came from its fill.

In the north-eastern corner of Area B was gully or ditch 10017, which was 10 m in length and aligned north-west to south-east (Fig. 3.1). Within its south-eastern terminal were 107 sherds of Middle Bronze Age Trevisker Ware, probably from a single vessel (see Mepham, Chapter 5, Fig. 5.1, 1–2). The terminal also contained a relatively large amount of burnt stone, not found in any of the other ditches or gullies.

Ditch 10016 was aligned on a similar north-west to south-east axis. It terminated to the south-east but continued beyond the limit of excavation to the north-west. Although gully 10016 contained five sherds of medieval pottery the alignment of it, broadly parallel to 10017, was at odds with the later medieval ditch alignments, suggesting gully 10016 may also be Bronze Age in date and the pottery intrusive. To the west, a further similarly aligned but undated gully, 10056, may have been contemporary with 10016 and 10017.

These gullies and ditches hint at some delineation of the landscape within this area during the Middle Bronze Age. The quantity of Trevisker Ware, along with the burnt stones, suggests a deliberate placement of material within the terminal of gully 10017. This activity may be related to the proximity of a palaeochannel – and perhaps springs in the vicinity – and may reflect Bronze Age practices of deposition in 'watery' locations. Alternatively, the stones may represent the remains of a burnt mound associated with boiling water either for cooking or for a prehistoric sauna.

Late Bronze Age–Middle Iron Age

A number of features in Area A are undated or contained minimal dating evidence (Fig. 3.2). However, their nature and some of the material found in the vicinity tentatively suggest that they are of Late Bronze Age–Early Iron Age date, though the use of some may have continued into the Middle Iron Age.

The south-east corner of a possible enclosure was revealed in the western half of Area A, comprising narrow, shallow ditches 10000, 10001 and 10009. Ditch 10000, 1–1.5 m wide and generally less than 0.5 m deep, was 65 m long and ran in a WSW to ENE direction and then turned northwards at its eastern end, where it continued beyond the limit of excavation. At its western end it intersected with ditch 10009 which continued for 4 m to the north before it terminated. A gap of 4.7 m between the junction of 10000 and 10009 and ditch 10001, which continued the east–west line of ditch 10000, may have been an entrance in the south side of the enclosure. A short length of gully (124) to the north may have been of

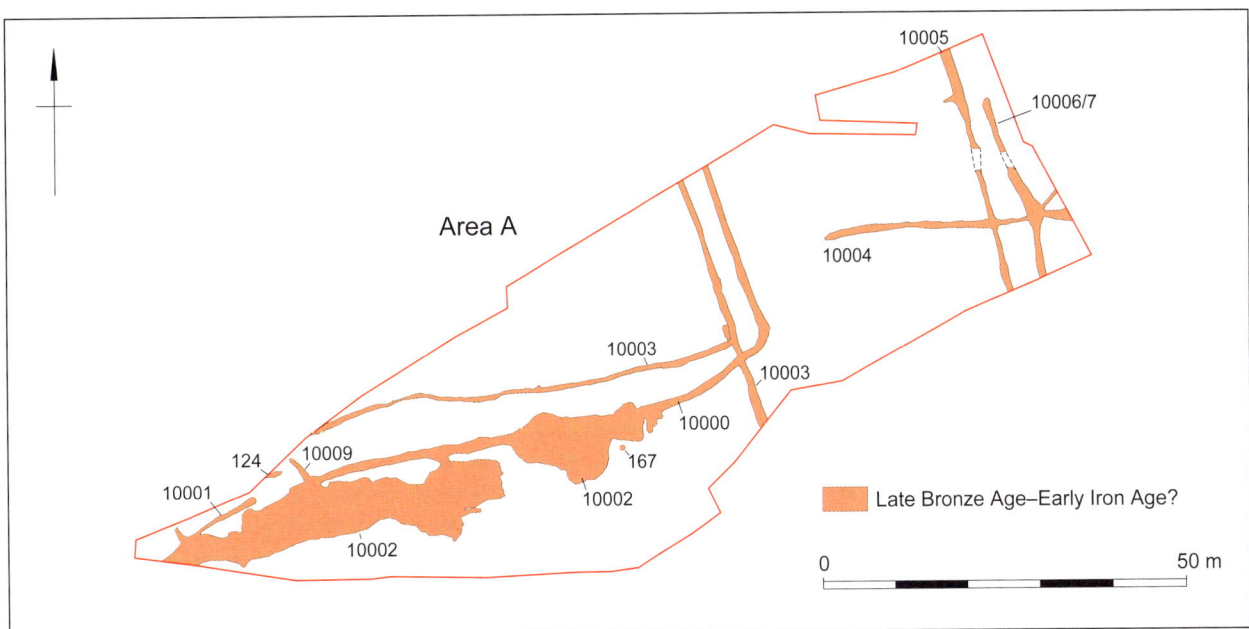

Figure 3.2 Prehistoric features in Area A

Figure 3.3 Prehistoric features in Areas C and D

similar date and was perhaps associated with the entrance. Other than this gully the possible enclosure was devoid of any internal features. Ditches 10000 and 10009 produced only a few pieces of struck flint/chert and burnt quartzite, though the former also contained a single small sherd of post-medieval pottery, which was probably intrusive.

A further, generally smaller ditch, 10003, may have been related to the enclosure. It was approximately parallel to and on the inside of ditch 10000, with a gap between them of 4–7.5m, before it turned at its eastern end to the NNW, with a possibly contemporary extension to the south. Together with 10000 and 10001 these features may have formed a double-ditched enclosure with external dimensions of at least 90 m by 25 m. However, the southern extension of ditch 10003 intersected with ditch 10000 (no relationship was discernible), suggesting that more than one phase is represented.

Towards the western end of the area feature 10002 lay parallel to and often merged with ditches 10000 and 10001, becoming more ephemeral at its eastern end. At its western end it continued beyond the limit of excavation. It was very irregular in plan, the depth varying greatly from 0.03 to 0.43 m. This and its undulating base suggest that the feature had resulted from erosion caused by overflow of water from ditch 10000, though some erosion may have resulted from trampling by animals or people. Feature 10002 contained 13 sherds of flint-tempered prehistoric (Late Bronze Age–Middle Iron Age) pottery, most of which were found close together,

Figure 3.4 Medieval features in Area B

suggesting the material came from a single vessel or deposit. The feature also contained a flint scraper and a core.

On the eastern side of the area was a further group of undated ditches and gullies (10004–7) which lay on a similar alignment to ditches 10000 and 10003 to the west. This suggests they were of a similar date and formed parts of related enclosures or field systems, also of more than one phase. Ditch 10006 was recut by ditch 10007, with ditch 10005 approximately parallel and 3.5–5 m to the west. Together they may have defined a trackway 35 m east of the possible double-ditched enclosure.

Within Area D a single isolated shallow gully (10014) was aligned WNW to ESE (Fig. 3.3). It contained two small abraded sherds of probable Bronze Age pottery which may have been residual. The gully extended from the eastern baulk for approximately 8.3 m before terminating to the west. Its different alignment to other, nearby features (see for example, Fig. 3.13) adds weight to the possibility of it being a prehistoric gully.

Iron Age and Romano-British Material

The Iron Age and Romano-British periods were very poorly represented. In Area B the truncated remains of possible pit 380 contained four sherds of Early Iron Age pottery; however it also contained two sherds of 12th- to 13th-century pottery, and it seems most likely that the 0.08 m deep feature was of medieval date.

Romano-British material was limited to 12 sherds of pottery, including two sherds of samian ware, found within Areas A and B. All of this is likely to have been residual and no features of this date were identified.

Period 2: Medieval

The principal discovery was the remains of a high status medieval building complex, located in the western half of Area B, with the surviving foundations indicating that this covered an area measuring approximately 40 m east–west by 30 m north–south (Fig. 3.4). Although heavily robbed, key elements within the stone building have been fairly certainly identified through comparison with other medieval manor house sites. These include a hall, a solar with garderobe (and perhaps a private chapel), and service quarters. There was an adjacent courtyard or service court to the south with at least one ancillary building and a possible detached kitchen. To the north was evidence for a walled forecourt and to the east was a series of enclosures.

There was a very restricted range and number of medieval finds, but together these suggest that occupation of the building complex spanned the late 12th or early 13th century to probably the late 14th or possibly the early 15th century. However, documentary research has failed to identify the owners and any records relating specifically to this building complex.

A series of Room numbers (1–10) has been allocated to facilitate description below and reference to Figure 3.4, which illustrates the principal components of the complex. The rooms are described spatially rather than in numerical order.

Early Features

As far as could be ascertained, the earliest feature of medieval date was ditch 10055, which extended north–south beneath Room 2 of the building complex (Fig. 3.4). It was almost 17 m long, continuing beyond the limit of excavation to the north, and was 1.75 m wide and 0.5 m deep. A small assemblage of 11th–13th-century pottery was recovered from the fill. The overall arrangement and sequence in this area is uncertain, but the ditch was cut by wall foundation 729, a probable buttress at the western end of the north wall of the hall (Room 3), though possibly also forming part of the solar block structure (Rooms 1 and 2; see below). Therefore, either ditch 10055 predated the solar block at the west end and was associated with an existing hall, or it pre-dated the entire medieval building complex. On balance, the latter is considered more likely, with the ditch representing an earlier land division or drainage feature, though some probable construction debris at its southern end suggests that it was still partly open and was then filled and levelled when construction of the medieval complex began. No other medieval features were identified that were certainly earlier than the buildings, though shallow hollow 10081, within and on the north side of the hall, may predate them.

The Building Complex

The northern part of the complex (Rooms 1–8, Fig. 3.4) was represented by a rectilinear arrangement of foundation trenches, much of the stone from which had been robbed (Pl. 3.3). Nonetheless, the majority of the plan of this part of the building complex was reasonably clear or could be extrapolated with some confidence (Fig. 3.5). The southern part of the complex was generally much better preserved (particularly the east of Room 10), having been subjected to less robbing, and in this area a slightly greater depth of overburden above the wall foundations served to protect them to some degree from subsequent plough damage.

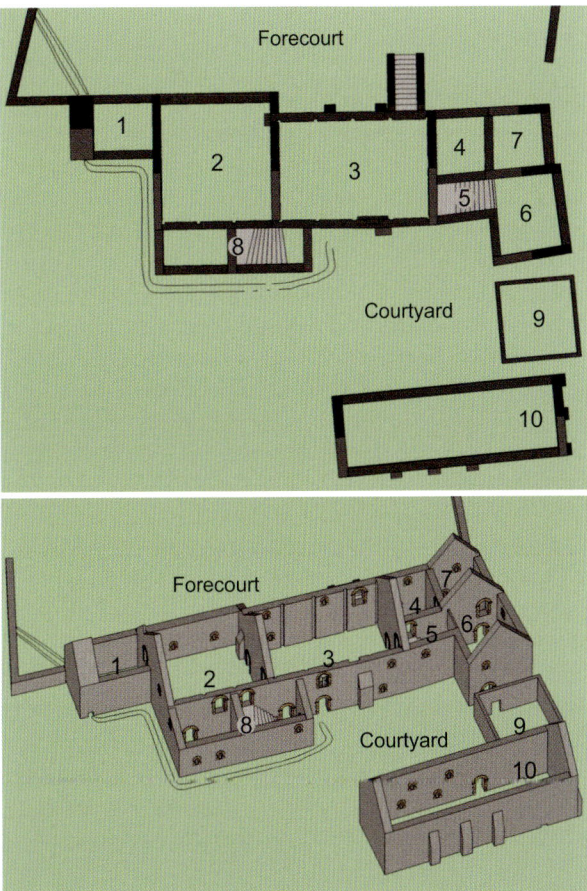

Figure 3.5 Reconstructed layout of medieval manor house

Plate 3.3 Overview of excavations in progress, with forecourt in foreground, solar area in centre, hall area to left, from north

Nine rooms were identified, with one more suggested by less complete wall lengths. The north range and the single surviving building on the southern side were arranged around a central courtyard or service court, approximately 12 m across and apparently open on the west side, though this was not confirmed. It is probable that a tenth room or building (Room 9) existed on the eastern side, between Rooms 6 and 10, although not enough of wall 10106 survived to allow certainty. A forecourt approximately 45 m wide lay in front of the north range, possibly enclosed by walls on the other three sides, but extending beyond the limit of excavation to the north.

The foundation trenches for the stone buildings were straight-sided and flat bottomed, generally approximately 1.2 m wide and 0.4 m deep, and packed fairly tightly with chert. This largely comprised chert nodules along the edges of the trenches, with a chert rubble core that also contained the occasional slab of Devonian shillet. In just one or two places remnants of walls of shillet survived above this level, though substantial parts of the wall foundations had been partly or in some places wholly removed by a later phase of systematic robbing. There were no obvious signs of mortar and it is possible that the chert was originally set in clay. The only evidence of lime mortar was located within part of wall 10047 (Room 8 – see below), which contained some white lime mortar in its southern side.

From around most of the wall foundations came stone roof-tile debris, the form and size of which suggests that virtually the entire complex was roofed with slates. A number of green-glazed ceramic crested ridge tiles were also found across the site, whilst a small number of glazed floor tiles came from the western end of the north range.

The north range

The north range appears to have been centred on Room 3, the large central space which is likely to have been the hall (Figs 3.4–5). To the west of Room 3, the plan is a little less clear, but three rooms have been identified (Rooms 1, 2 and 8), almost certainly comprising the solar block, the principal living accommodation. To the east of Room 3 were Rooms 4 and 5, which it is suggested were service rooms, as were probably Rooms 6 and 7 adjoining them at the east end of the building.

Room 3 – the hall

Room 3 was located in the centre of the north range, and measured 12 by 7.5 m (Figs 3.4–6). The position, size and shape of the room suggest that it was the Great Hall, and the width (up to 1.4 m) and depth (up to 0.45 m) of the foundations indicate that

Figure 3.6 Visualisation of north elevation of manor house

Plate 3.4 Wall foundation 10077 – west wall of hall, from north-east

it was of substantial construction, possibly of two storeys, perhaps with the hall at first floor level. Wall foundation 10067 marked the south side, wall 10077 the west side (Pl. 3.4), and wall 10079 the north and east sides, the latter continuing around the north-east corner of the building without a break indicating that these two walls belonged to a single phase of construction. It is likely that all the walls were built at the same time, but the relationships at the north-west and south-west corners had been rendered unclear as a result of subsequent stone robbing. Wall foundation 729 at the western end of the north wall was somewhat larger than the adjacent foundations and appears to have formed the base of a buttress at the north-west corner of the hall (Pl. 3.5), though how this buttress articulated with the solar to the west is unclear. The hall had at least two other external buttresses, on the north and south sides (1085 and 791 respectively; Pl. 3.6), with the almost completely robbed remains of possibly another on the north side,

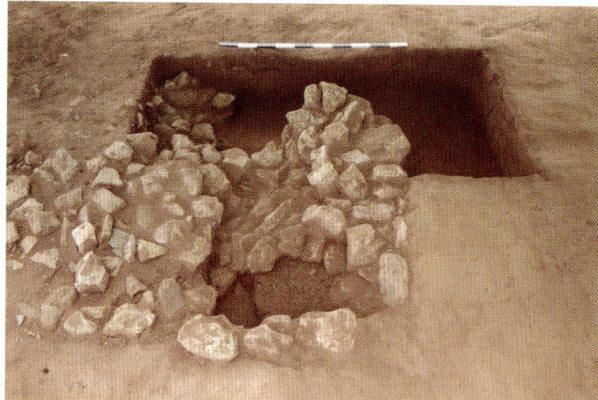

Plate 3.5 Hall buttress 729, from north

Plate 3.6 Hall buttresses a) 1085, from south; b) 791, from east

4 m to the east of 1085. However, this possible buttress may have been associated with wall foundation 686 (see below), whilst a shallow pit (10082) containing a few sherds of 11th–13th-century pottery on the inside of the north wall here was presumably the remains of an internal feature. Immediately to the west of this was a thin spread of soil which filled a poorly defined, shallow hollow (10081), initially interpreted as a possible tree-throw hole. As a result of later robbing, it was unclear if the north wall of the hall cut hollow 10081, or if the material in the hollow had accumulated after the construction of the wall. However, this deposit contained a relatively large assemblage (26 sherds) of 11th–13th-century pottery, some pieces quite large and unabraded.

No surfaces survived within Room 3, and there was no clear evidence for the locations of a hearth or fireplace. The apparent lack of a central hearth might support the suggestion of a first floor hall, and it is possible that buttress 791 on the south side may have been associated with a wall fireplace at this level. The function of buttress 1085 and its possible neighbour on the north wall is unclear, other than as simply structural features, as it is unlikely that there would have been a fireplace here, adjacent to the presumed hall entrance immediately to the east.

Two short lengths of wall foundation, 686 and 1030, 1.25 m apart and just over 5 m long, were located to the north of Room 3. Both had been heavily robbed, and wall 1030 further damaged by a field drain and wall 686 also disturbed. The walls lay at 90° to the building, and it is suggested that they may have formed part of an external staircase to the postulated first floor hall, forming the principal entrance on the north side from the forecourt. The location of an entrance here, at the east end of the hall, would probably place the high end of the hall at the west end, adjacent to the solar.

Rooms 1, 2 and 8 – the solar
Room 2 lay immediately to the west of Room 3 and measured approximately 8.5 m square. Wall 10077 to the east was shared with Room 3, with fragmentary foundation 1462 on the south side and foundations 1006 and 10074 to the west, the latter the less heavily robbed of the two. The reason for the offset and apparent gap (of 4 m) in the north wall between foundations 1491 and 10079 is not easily resolved, and their relationship to each other is further complicated by partly robbed wall foundation 729, a relatively substantial survival which appears to have formed part of a buttress at the west end of the north wall of the hall. However, it is suggested that Room 2 formed the core of the solar block, of two storeys, and comprised the principal chamber at first floor level (Figs 3.4–5), with direct access from the high (west)

Figure 3.7 Plan of garderobe

end of the hall. A small area of tightly packed chert (678; not illustrated) may have been the remnants of a cobbled surface at ground floor level, or possibly the foundation of an internal dividing wall. A narrow, shallow foundation, 1950, projecting from the south wall could also have been part of such a division, which would have partitioned off a space 3 m wide at the east end.

Fragments of decorated floor tiles from the vicinity of Room 2 (none were found *in situ*) are dated to the 14th century (see Mepham, Chapter 4), and their presence here adds further weight to the interpretation that this end of the building was of higher status, commensurate with the solar having been located here.

Room 1 was located at the western end of the north range, beyond Room 2. It measured 4.9 by 3.6 m and may have served as the bedchamber at first floor level. The wall foundations and robber cuts on the north and south sides (10061 and 10058 respectively) were substantial – up to 1 m wide and 0.55 m deep – providing further confirmation that this part of the building is likely to have had an upper storey. Wall 10048 on the west side was different, and the width and nature of its construction (described further below) indicates that it incorporated the drain for a garderobe on the first floor, with access that allowed it to be cleaned out at ground level from the south side (Fig. 3.7). Drain 10044 extended around the southern side of the solar block and fed into the

Plate 3.7 Base of garderobe 10048, from south

Plate 3.8 Room 8 in foreground, with solar area (left) and hall area (right) behind, from south

base of the garderobe from the south (and extended to the north through the forecourt), perhaps serving to periodically help flush it out (Pl. 3.7).

The north wall foundation (10061) of Room 1 extended a further 5 m to the west (as 960), interrupted by the presence of wall 10048 forming part of the garderobe block, before turning to continue northwards beyond the limit of excavation. The northern continuation (769) was of slightly different construction and was not faced with flat chert like the remainder. This, the angle of the wall and the apparent lack of a return suggest that it formed part of a boundary wall, in this case bounding the west side of a forecourt to the complex (see Pl. 3.14).

To the south of Room 2 was Room 8, a relatively narrow space measuring 2.75 m wide by 11.4 m long (Pl. 3.8). The foundations had been heavily robbed but wall 10047 defined the south side and appears to have been of the same build as wall 1006 of Room 2; the relationship to wall foundation 10067, the south wall of the hall, was not clear. Room 8 may also have been of two storeys and, it is suggested below, could have accommodated steps providing private access to the solar from the courtyard, and perhaps also a chapel at first floor level with a direct link between this and Room 2 to the north (Fig. 3.8).

Rooms 4–7 and 9 – the service range

Immediately east of the hall (Room 3) were Rooms 4 and 5 (Figs 3.4–5). The outer wall foundations were continuous with those of Room 3, but those of the internal dividing walls, 10086 and 10087, were somewhat shallower. The location and size of the two rooms suggest that they served a service function, providing a buttery and perhaps storage space that was probably spread over two levels. Room 4 measured 3.8 by 3.5 m, whilst Room 5 was somewhat smaller at 3.8 by 1.85 m. In the north-west corner of Room 4 was a gap of 0.55 m (1047), indicating the possible location of a doorway between this and Room 3 at ground floor level.

At the eastern end of the north range were Rooms 6 and 7 (Figs 3.4–5), the evidence suggesting, despite extensive robbing of the foundations, that together these formed a later addition to the building. In plan they appear to represent a cross wing, continuing the line of the building along the north side but extending

Figure 3.8 Visualisation of south elevation of hall, solar and entrance from courtyard

Figure 3.9 Visualisation of service range, detached kitchen and east end of ancillary building

it by 4 m to the south (Fig. 3.9). This perhaps included further service rooms and storage space, though the possibility is considered below that there was a re-arrangement at this end of the building in order to provide more guest accommodation.

Room 7, the smaller of the two, was located at the north-east corner of the building. It was square, measuring approximately 4.5 by 4.5 m, and the surviving wall foundations on the northern and eastern sides, 10089, were relatively shallow in comparison to those on the western side. This provides further evidence that this room was part of a later extension, possibly of single storey height, though perhaps of two storeys and partly built of timber, at least above ground floor level. No internal features survived other than a short length of narrow, shallow gully, 10090, aligned north–south.

Room 6 was directly to the south of Room 7 and measured approximately 6.4 m long by 4.5 m wide, the width suggesting that it may have projected a little further to the east than Room 7, though there is nothing to indicate that they were not of contemporary construction. Wall foundations 807 and 806 marked the south and west sides respectively, and 808 marked the north-east corner and part of the east side. The return of wall 808 to the west corresponds with the line of the foundation, 10087, dividing Rooms 4 and 5, though whether this was coincidental is unclear. Within the centre of Room 6 were the remnants of a possible hearth, 10098, an area of heat-affected ground and with some associated charcoal flecking. However, there was no surviving hearth structure, nor the remains of any associated floor surface. The possibility is considered below that Room 6 may have been a kitchen during the latest phase of use of the building, and the recovery of charred cleaned grain from layer 725 within this room might support this interpretation (see Wyles, Chapter 6), or at least that foodstuffs may have been stored here.

Immediately to the north of Room 7 of the added cross wing was an approximately right-angled arrangement of wall foundations (728 and 952) and a short length of ditch (10042), the latter apparently the earliest element (Fig. 3.4). Together these appear to have defined the eastern side of the forecourt, as well as forming an entrance to this from the enclosures beyond to the east. Wall 728 was on the same alignment as wall 769 to the west of the forecourt, the foundation surviving as a single course of stones in a trench 0.75 m wide.

Room 9 lay to the south of Room 6 of the cross wing, separated from it by a gap of a little under 1.5 m (Figs 3.4–5). Very little of this structure survived, in large part because the walls were relatively insubstantial, the main element being right-angled wall 10106, which is thought to have defined the south-east corner (Pl. 3.9). Wall 10106 was aligned west to east before turning at its eastern end and continuing north towards the south-east corner of Room 6. The northern and western sides of Room 9 had been almost completely destroyed by robbing and truncation, only 1295 surviving on the west side, with nothing to the north. This and the absence of any surviving internal features makes interpretation difficult. However, it is possible that Room 9 was a

Plate 3.9 Detached kitchen (Room 9) – wall 10106, with Room 6 in background, and walls 1403 and 10103 to right, from south-east

detached kitchen, approximately 6 m square, on the east side of the courtyard between the service end of the north range and the south range (Fig. 3.9). Such a structure is likely to have been built largely of timber, open to the eaves, with walls of wattle and daub, but here there is insufficient evidence to speculate further.

Two short (2.5–3 m long) but relatively broad and apparently free-standing lengths of wall, 1403 and 10103, lay parallel to the eastern walls of Rooms 9 and 6 respectively (see Pl. 3.9). Their purpose is unclear and they may have been associated with ancillary structures within the enclosure immediately to the east, accessed via a passageway between Rooms 6 and 9 (see below).

The south range

Room 10 comprised a relatively long, narrow building at the eastern end of the south range, possibly the only building in this range, the extent of which is unclear (Figs 3.4–5; Pl. 3.10). It most probably represents an ancillary building, lying on the south side of the courtyard or service court. The southern wall, 10040, was up to 1 m wide, and from the south-eastern corner it was traced westwards for a total distance of approximately 15 m, gradually diminishing in height from a maximum of 0.95 m until it survived only intermittently; how far it originally continued beyond this to the west is unknown (Fig. 3.10). Six sherds of 14th–15th-century pottery came from the soil associated with wall 10040, but probably not from the foundation trench itself. There were two buttresses on the outside of wall 10040, and possibly a third which had been largely destroyed. There was also a step up in the foundations of this wall, 5.2 m from the south-east corner (see Pl. 3.11), the deeper footings here suggesting that the east end of the building was more substantial than elsewhere. The east end of the building was defined by wall 1038, which indicated the building to have been 5 m wide internally, and the bases of two further possible buttresses, 1426 and 1516, sat against the outer face of the wall at the east end. The western extent of the northern element of wall 1038, at just over 5 m long, matched that of the deeper foundations present at the east end of wall 10040 to the south. This, the presence of the buttresses, the thickness of the walls and the greater depth of the foundations here suggest that the building may have been two storeys in height, at least at the east end, and perhaps this part was wholly built in stone. To the west of wall 1038 only a short length of north wall 695 remained, and this appeared to be a later addition. It was offset slightly to the north, was of less substantial construction and had shallower foundations than wall 1038 (see Pl. 3.12). Beyond this, the western part of the building may have been open fronted, although it is perhaps more likely that the foundations here were relatively shallow, perhaps supporting a timber superstructure, and in this area have been entirely truncated.

The principal internal feature within Room 10 was drain 10071, a substantial and well-constructed feature that ran north–south across the eastern end

Plate 3.10 Overview of excavations in progress, with ancillary building 10 in foreground, from south-east

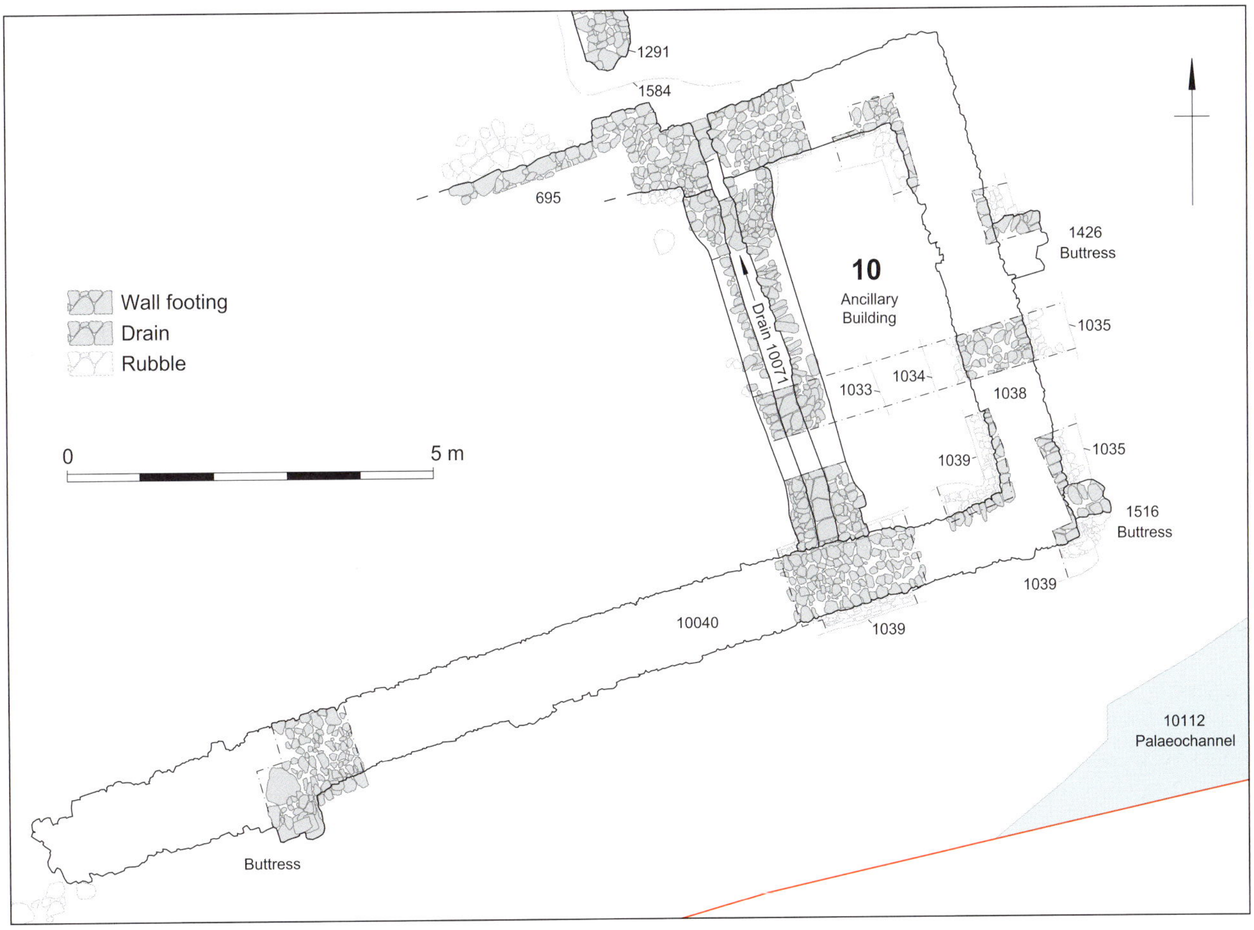

Figure 3.10 Plan of ancillary building

and comprised two chert-built walls with a slate-lined base (Fig. 3.10). The drain was keyed into and extended through the northern and southern walls, 1038 and 10040 respectively (Pls 3.11–12), and on the inside of the south wall there was a step in the base. Palaeochannel 10112 (see below) lay just to the south of the building, and the difference in levels suggests that, contrary to expectation, water from the palaeochannel could have been drained from this, through the building and out of the north side into the courtyard. There was no surviving ditch or gully on the outside (Pl. 3.13) and no indication of where the water went when it reached the courtyard, though it is possible that a trough or similar feature for collecting water may have been located adjacent to the north wall of Room 10. The step in the base of the

Plate 3.11 Drain 10071 within ancillary building/Room 10; south wall 10040 (note shallower wall foundations to right), from north

Plate 3.14 Drain 10044 around exterior of Room 8, from south-west

Plate 3.12 Drain 10071 in ancillary building/Room 10; external exit through north wall 1038 into courtyard (note offset of wall 695 to right), from north

Plate 3.13 Drain 10071 in ancillary building/Room 10; external opening through south wall 10040, from south

drain may indicate that it could be opened or blocked off as required, though the precise mechanism for water control is unclear, as is whether the water was intended for a specific purpose rather than simply providing a supply for general use.

A charcoal-rich deposit, 690, survived at the east end of the building, suggesting at least one burning episode took place within Room 10, but no floor surfaces survived, nor was there any evidence for internal divisions. Charred cereal grain recovered from deposit 690 is indicative of waste from stored grain (see Wyles, Chapter 6), similar to that found in Room 6.

Drainage

Drainage was an important aspect of the medieval building complex and evidence of water management was present in various places across this part of the site.

The most obvious remains comprised a rubble-filled chert-lined drain, 10044, just over 30 m in length, located just outside the southern side of the west end of the northern wing (Pl. 3.14). From close to the south-west corner of Room 3 it extended around the exterior of Room 8 and part of Room 2, and then along the southern side of Room 1, at which point the chert-lined section ended (see Fig. 3.4). The difference in levels between the east and west ends of drain 10044 (49.7 m OD and 49.3 m OD respectively) confirm that water would have flowed westwards away from Room 3, and eventually passed into a drain incorporated within wall foundation 10048 in Room 1 at the western end of the building, part of the solar block.

The size, nature and quality of construction of wall foundation 10048 indicate that this section of the drain, which ran from south to north, formed part of

Plate 3.15 Base of garderobe 10048, from south-east

Plate 3.16 Detail of base of garderobe 10048, from south

Plate 3.17 Forecourt, south-west corner, with wall 769 to right and drain 10117 from garderobe to left, from north-west

the basal element of a garderobe (Pl. 3.15). Overall, the base of the garderobe measured 5.8 m long and 2.6 m wide, and survived to a height of 0.85 m. It comprised a substantial double-stepped rubble foundation, the steps up to a maximum height of 0.42 m and 0.23 m respectively, and each between 0.1 m and 0.16 m wide. The drain running through it was 0.5 m wide, the base consisting of flat slabs of sandstone set on top of the rubble foundation, and the southern end had an arched opening, partly collapsed and largely robbed, constructed of chert and the occasional slate roof tile on edge (Pl. 3.16). At its southern end the level of the drain was 49.33 m OD and at its northern it was 49.37 m OD, the minor difference in height probably a result of subsidence. The garderobe base was cut by later ditch 10059, but it was noticeably less heavily robbed than other parts of the building complex, despite providing a readily available source of stone, none of it apparently mortared.

At the northern end of wall foundation 10048 the drain exited the garderobe block and turned to the north-west, crossing the south-west corner of the forecourt and continuing beyond the limit of excavation (Pl. 3.17). This portion of drain 10117 was also relatively large and well-constructed, lined with chert, though there were no stones forming the base and no remains of any stone cover, though it seems likely one would have been present originally.

Two further chert-lined drains, 10052 and 10054, lay to the north of Room 1, both aligned in a northerly direction and extending beyond the limits of excavation. The junctions between the two drains and wall 1491 suggested that they were broadly contemporary, though they perhaps served different purposes, one drain taking water from the roof of the solar and the other from the ground floor, for example. A similar drain, 10101, extended along part of the east side of Room 6 and presumably took water from the roof of the extended service wing.

Associated Enclosures

To the east of the medieval building complex in Area B was a series of ditches and gullies which appear to have defined three distinct but related groups of enclosures, one adjacent to the building and another 25 m or so to the east, with a third occupying the space between them (Fig. 3.11). Individual ditches

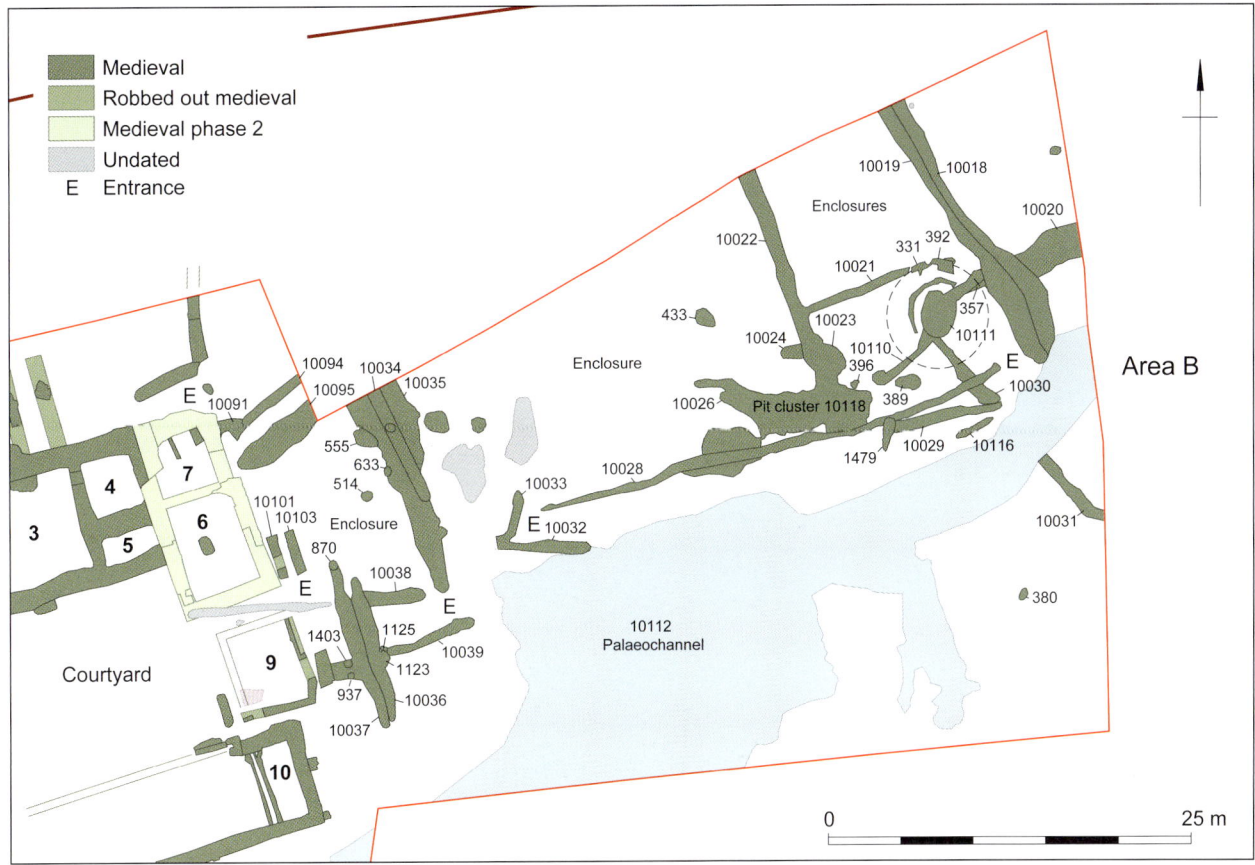

Figure 3.11 Plan of medieval features to east of manor house

and gullies varied considerably in size, with widths varying between 0.4 and 2.35 m and depths ranging from 0.1 to 0.45 m.

Western group

The group of ditches adjacent to the building appeared to define a small sub-rectangular enclosure, of at least two phases, measuring a maximum of 20 m north–south by 10 m east–west. The northern extent corresponded with that of the main building complex, and the enclosure appears to have been laid out as an extension of the courtyard/service court. Access into this enclosure was through the passageway between Rooms 6 and 9 (the later extension to the service wing and the detached kitchen respectively), with an opening to the area beyond through a 2 m wide opening at the south-east corner. Pottery from the enclosure ditches is of 14th–15th-century date, and probably broadly contemporary with the use of the newly extended service wing.

On the east side was a relatively broad, shallow ditch, 10035, recut by a narrower ditch, 10034, the corresponding ditches on the north side probably comprising 10095 and 10094 respectively. Ditch 10095 contained a relatively large amount of late medieval pottery (including sherds from two costrels – see Fig. 5.2, 8; Pl. 5.1) along with a single post-medieval sherd, and both ditches were cut by post-medieval ditch 10093 (see Fig. 3.12). Ditch 10091, perhaps an extension of 10094, was cut at its western end by the robber trench associated with wall foundation 10089 (Room 7), and also contained late medieval pottery. Ditch 10039, extending from the detached kitchen, defined the south side of the enclosure, and this was not recut. Ditch 10038 crossed this enclosure at an angle and may have been a drainage feature extending from the south-west corner of Room 6 (part of the extension to the service range) to the south-east entrance to the enclosure. Both 10038 and ditch 10039 had been cut by a pair of adjacent, possibly recut ditches, 10036 and 10037, 10 m and 12 m long respectively. The function of these two later ditches is unclear, though they may relate to the second phase of ditches to the west and north (10034 and 10094 respectively). Overall, where dated by pottery, all of the ditches in this group can be assigned to the 14th century, with evidence for continuity into at least the early 15th century.

Within the area were at least seven pits, some (eg, 555 and 1125) relatively early in the sequence, some (eg, 633, 870 and 937) later and others (eg, 514 and 1123) uncertainly placed. However, pottery dating suggests that most, if not all, belong to the 11th–13th century, earlier than the ditches here. The pits varied

Plate 3.18 Overview of excavations in progress, with medieval pit complex to right and palaeochannel 10112 to left, with manor house in background, from south-east

in shape and size but were generally small, 0.4–1.5 m across and 0.1–0.6 m deep. In addition to a few sherds of pottery, some contained small amounts of animal bone, but others were devoid of finds. Of note, however, is the presence in several pits and ditches, both here and to the east, of relatively large assemblages of charred plant remains, specifically threshing waste, indicative of crop processing (see Wyles, Chapter 6).

Eastern group
The eastern group of enclosures can be divided in to two phases on stratigraphic grounds, though the pottery from both phases can only be assigned a broad 11th–13th-century date. However, this group of enclosures does seem to predate the western group of ditches (see above), which are assigned to the 14th–early 15th century.

The earliest phase of the eastern group appears to comprise the north-west corner of a possible rectangular enclosure, which was cut by several later features. The north side was defined by ditch 357 and probably also 10110 and 10020, with ditches 10030 and 10031 on the west side. Ditch 10030 appears to have respected palaeochannel 10112, though 10031 to the south-east was apparently cut by it; perhaps this was a result of later erosion on this side of the channel. Ditch 10031 and pit 380 to the south-west of it were the only features exposed to the south of the palaeochannel in this area.

The second phase of enclosures and related features were confined to the north side of palaeochannel 10112. The principal element comprised a rectangular enclosure approximately 10 m wide and at least 20 m long, extending south-east to north-west, on the same alignment as the earlier enclosure and at right angles to the palaeochannel. Ditch 10019 on the east side was recut by 10018, with ditch 10222 defining the west side. Ditch 10029 may have initially formed the south side, with gaps at the south-east and south-west corners. It is suggested that this was subsequently replaced by ditch 10028, which extended further to the west than its predecessor, thereby forming the south side of the central enclosure, which lay between those to the east and west (see below). There was a 2 m wide entrance at the south-east corner of the eastern enclosure, between ditches 10019 and 10028, and 10021 formed an internal division, with a gap between this ditch and 10019 creating an access point between the northern and southern parts of the enclosure.

No features were exposed within the northern part of the enclosure, but several lay in the smaller, southern part, which measured approximately 10 by 8 m. These included two relatively large shallow pits, 389 and 1479, the latter cutting ditch 10028.

Pit 1479 was irregularly shaped and 389 sub-oval, but both were shallow and flat bottomed. Pit 1479 measured 4.4 by 1.8 m and was 0.25 m deep, whilst pit 389 was 3.8 m long, 2.9 m wide and 0.3 m deep. Pit 479 produced just two sherds of 11th–13th-century pottery, and pit 389 is undated. The function of these pits is unclear, but their position towards the corner of the enclosure might suggest that they were temporary watering holes, their somewhat irregular shape a result of trampling by animals.

Also in the south-west corner of the eastern enclosure was a large cluster of pits, 10118, which extended for almost 10 m across into the central enclosure (Pl. 3.18). These, pits 10023 and 10024 and others nearby, may have been small clay quarries as they were located within an area where the natural had a notably higher clay content than elsewhere. They varied in shape, size and depth, all being between 0.4 and 2.4 m across, and most were relatively shallow, with depths of 0.1–0.6 m. Three of these pits, 10023, 10025 and 10027 (both the latter part of 10118), contained 11th–13th-century pottery (six, three and 35 sherds respectively), and while several cut enclosure ditch 10022 others appeared to be cut by ditch 10028.

At least five postholes were located within the pit cluster, with a further example (396) to the north-east. Two of the postholes contained chert packing, but no structure could be discerned amongst them.

On the east side within the southern part of the eastern enclosure, and probably contemporary with it, was a rather enigmatic structure that appears to have been heavily plough damaged and to have survived only in part (Fig. 3.11). Stratigraphically the earliest element may have been 10111, a central, shallow, oval hollow measuring approximately 3 by 2.5 m. This was surrounded on the north-west side by a narrow, curving gully, which if projected would have formed a circle with a diameter of 4.5 m. Outside of this on the north side were two fragments of wall, 331 and 392, which can be projected, admittedly somewhat speculatively, to form a circle of approximately 7 m diameter. The wall was constructed from the same materials, chert and shillett, as used in the other medieval buildings, 331 surviving only one stone wide and 392 to two stones width. The two fragments of wall were a maximum of two courses in height, neither was mortared, but gaps between the stones in 331 were filled with clay. The remains appear to all be part of a single structure, probably relatively insubstantial, and serving an agricultural purpose. A dovecote is a possibility, but more substantial foundations would be anticipated, and it is perhaps more likely to have been a pigsty or some other walled enclosure to contain and house animals.

Central group

The central enclosure lay between the ditches defining the enclosures to the east and the west, with ditch 10028 bounding the southern side. These enclosed an area approximately 28 m wide and at least 15 m long, extending to the north beyond the limit of excavation. There was a gap at the south-west corner, with ditches 10032 and 10033 possibly forming part of the entrance arrangements here. There were a few pits inside including 433 and 10024, with part of pit cluster 10118 extending into the south-east corner. A broad, shallow depression, (10026, possibly a watering hole, was located on the western side of the cluster (the relationship between them unclear), and this feature contained 19 sherds of 11th–13th-century pottery.

Palaeochannel 10112

This palaeochannel lay to the south of the building complex and the associated enclosures to the west (Figs 3.4 and 3.11; Pl. 3.18), and appears to have been active during the medieval period and probably later, most likely feeding into a fishpond (later called Hobby Pond) just over 100 m to the east. It ran in a south-west to north-east direction for 54 m within the excavation area, continuing in both directions beyond this. At its widest it was 17.5 m across, where it may have survived as or formed a small pond, narrowing to 5 m in the north-east. It was up to 0.55 m deep, with a rather irregular base, and largely filled with peaty material. Unfortunately, nothing of environmental significance was forthcoming from the fill, which contained some roof slate and chert from the demolition of the medieval building.

Other Ditches and Gullies

To the south of Area B, trench 56 (see Fig. 1.1) contained only two possible medieval features. A small north-east to south-west aligned ditch (877) contained five medieval sherds and was orientated in a similar direction to an undated ditch terminal, which may suggest both were of similar date. How precisely these features related to the medieval building complex to the north is unclear, though it is likely that they formed part of a contemporary enclosure or field system which lay to the south of palaeochannel 10112. The paucity of features in this area, compared to that to the east of the medieval building complex, indicates a relatively low density of enclosures/fields here, as highlighted by the earlier evaluation trenches.

Only three other medieval features were identified elsewhere on the site and these comprised three gullies, 276, 10015 and 10109, all at the western end

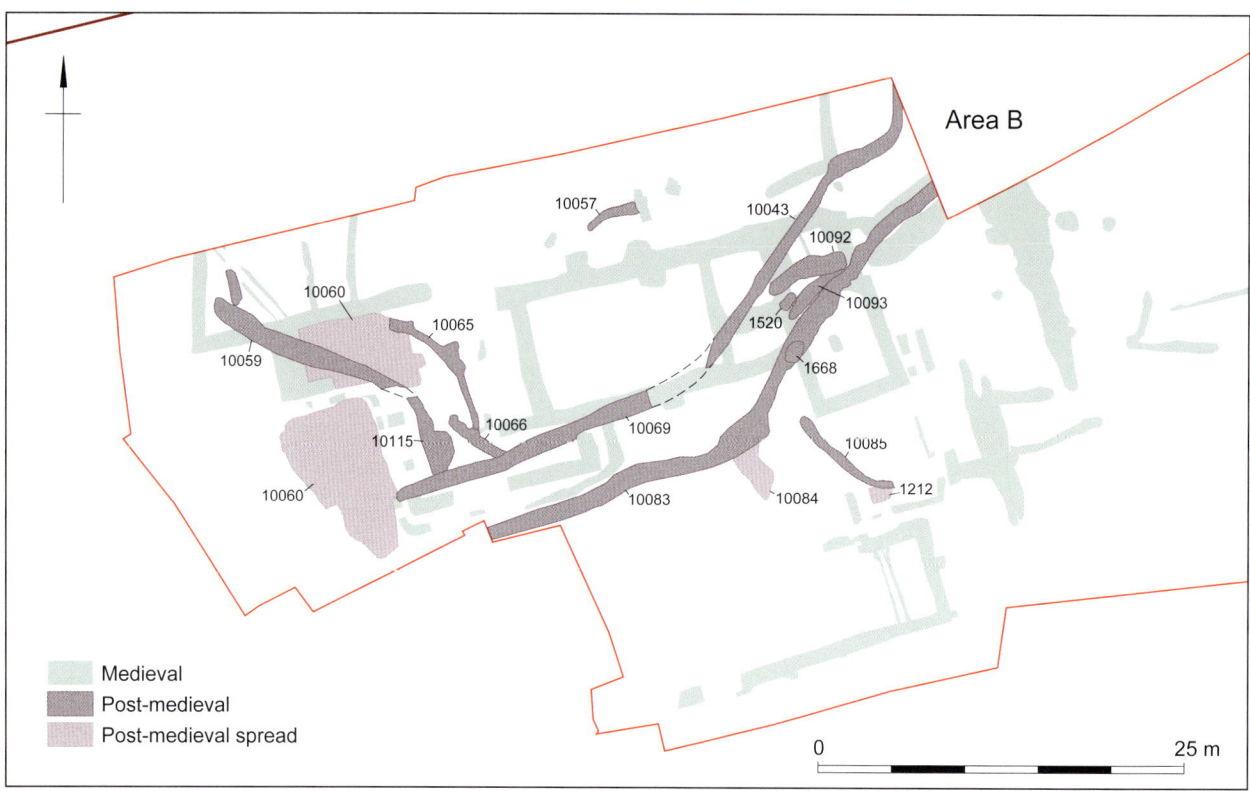

Figure 3.12 Plan of post-medieval features in area of manor house

of Area C (see Fig. 3.13). Gullies 10109 and 10015 were parallel to each other, but the relationship between 276 and 10109 was unclear. All three gullies contained 11th–13th-century pottery, including jar rims from 276 and 10109. Gullies 10015 and 10109 were traced for approximately 11 m, terminating to the south but continuing beyond the limit of excavation to the north. Both were just over 0.2 m deep, with gully 10015 up to 0.8 m wide and gully 10109 1.2 m wide. It is possible that these gullies were dug for drainage purposes, as they both terminated close to the lowest point within the area, though the pottery might indicate some settlement activity in the immediate vicinity of Area C.

Period 3 Later Medieval/Post-medieval

There were two main areas of later medieval and post-medieval activity, one within Area B and one covering Areas C and D. Dating evidence is extremely sparse, and it can only be surmised that activity spanned the 16th to the 19th centuries.

Area B

In stratigraphic terms, the earliest remains post-dating the medieval building were demolition deposits which filled a large, irregular depression, 10060, towards the western end of the area (Fig. 3.12). These were cut by ditch 10059 and possibly also by 10069, though the relationship was unclear. Another spread, 10084, was cut by ditch 10083. From these demolition deposits came six sherds of Tudor Green pottery, the only ones from the site, which conventionally is assigned to the 14th–late 15th/early 16th century.

Several ditches crossed Area B, the most substantial being 10043, 10069 and 10083, of which 10043 and 10069 belonged to a single, truncated ditch. This and ditch 10083 ran parallel, approximately 3.5 m apart, and extended north-east to south-west from the northern edge of the area before changing course in the centre to a more westerly direction. They crossed Rooms 3–8 of the medieval building, including some of the robber trenches, and perhaps defined a trackway that led towards the former route between Wellington and Nynehead, just to the west of Area B. This route fell into disuse during the 19th century, but is still marked as a footpath on the 1st edition of the 6" OS map.

Two short sections of ditch, 10092 and 10093, lay between ditches 10043 and 10083, ditch 10093 cut by both 10083 and 10092. Ditches 10092 and 10093 contained some building material, presumably from the demolition of the medieval buildings.

Ditch 10059, along with ditch 10066, aligned south-east to north-west, extended north from ditch 10069, which defined the north side of the possible

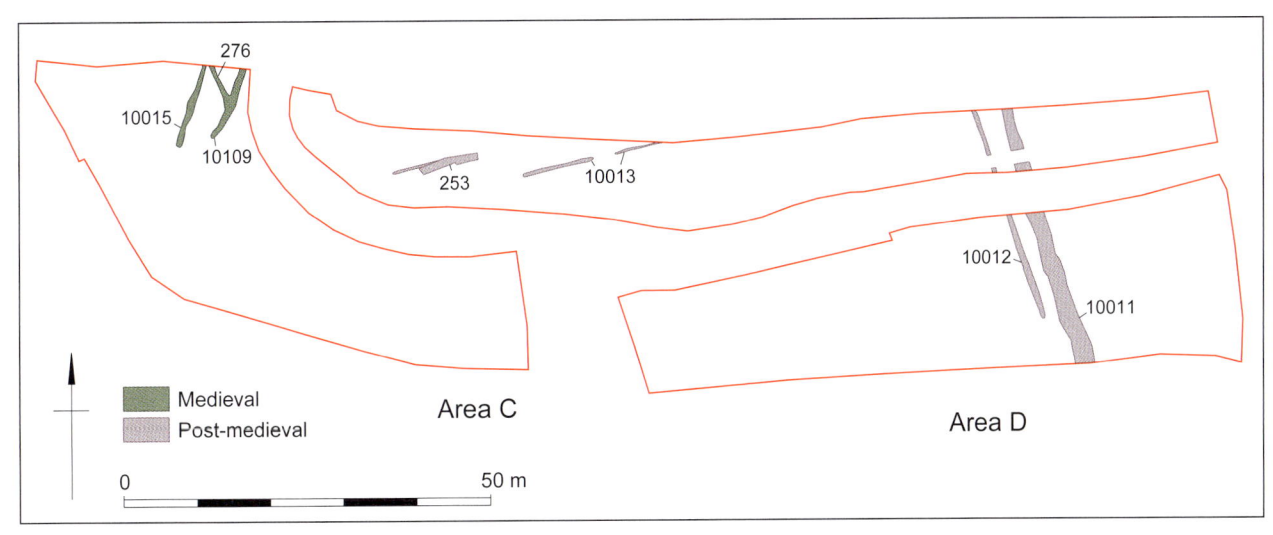

Figure 3.13 Plan of post-medieval features in Areas C and D

trackway, and cut through the western side of the medieval building complex, most notably the base of the garderobe block, as well as demolition spread 10060. However, ditch 10059 terminated before reaching medieval wall 769. On the west side of ditch 10066/10059 was a shallow cut, 10115, which contained demolition debris, and to the east was a curvilinear ditch, 10065, which also cut demolition spread 10060.

Elsewhere, a short length of gully, 10057, located in the north of Area B, contained building material as well as single sherds of medieval and post-medieval pottery and a fragment of clay pipe stem. Further to the south, gully 10085, aligned north-west to south-east, post-dated the medieval building and cut spread 1212.

Two small post-medieval pits, 1520 and 1668, lay within and appeared to post-date the possible trackway, pit 1520 containing some roofing slate.

Areas C and D

Several small ditches within Areas C and D represent the remnants of post-medieval field boundaries (Fig. 3.13). Ditches 10011 and 10012, aligned approximately NNW to SSE, crossed Areas C and D, parallel to each other and also to the modern field boundaries. Ditch 10012 terminated to the south, whereas 10011 continued beyond the limit of excavation. Ditch 10013, at right angles to these ditches, corresponds with a boundary shown on the tithe map.

The partial remains of an east to west wall (253) survived within Area D, on the same alignment and just to the north of ditch 10113. It was traced for at least 7.8 m and was up to 0.43 m wide, built of red brick and sub-rounded flint nodules bonded with a pale brown lime mortar. It is likely to have been the remains of an otherwise unrecorded farm building.

Chapter 4
Building Materials

Building Stone
by Bob Davis

Wellington is located on the border between Somerset and Devon. Geologically this is a mixed area with abundant building stone available. In her book *Traditional Houses of Somerset*, Jane Penoyre (2005, 11–12) states that the local stone is suitable mainly for plain walling, with most sources of freestone (stone that can be worked for dressings such as windows and doorways, ashlar masonry, mouldings and fireplaces) located further to the north-west.

Wellington lies in a region dominated by three geological zones, the oldest of which are the Devonian deposits to the west extending into Devon, consisting of upper deposits of sandstones, grits and slates. Triassic deposits of Marl and sandstones are found in the immediate area of Wellington, whilst Cretaceous deposits of Upper Greensand containing grit, chert and sandstones occur in the area to the south in the Blackdown Hills.

Foundations

By far, the most common building material recorded at Longforth Farm was chert, in the form of small to medium sized nodules, used in the foundations of all of the walls. What was noticeable, however, was the lack of any mortar binding the irregularly shaped stones, even in areas where significant sections of wall foundations survived. Instead they appeared to be earth-bound below ground level, and as virtually no walling remained above, it is not possible to speculate as to the binding matrix used here. It is entirely possible that, below ground, traditional lime mortar was not used, the chert nodules being set within a foundation trench and held together by compression of the weight of the walling above. This would have provided a strong, durable foundation, capable of resisting decay and disintegration as a result of the large compression forces created by the weight of the upper walling.

Walling

The lack of identifiable walling above ground level, resulting from comprehensive robbing, means it is difficult to speculate as to what the walls were constructed from. One piece of potential evidence is the few surviving pieces of Devonian 'shillet', which comprise roughly hewn, small slabs of greenish slatey rock. The size and shape of these pieces would suggest that they were used as walling because their various sizes would have allowed the wall thickness to be 'tied'. That is to say, larger pieces were set into the inner core of the wall with a single face side flush with the face of the wall. Their tabular nature also meant that little or no dressing was necessary.

Devonian shillet is found predominantly to the north-west of Wellington, and more specifically the Brendon Hills and Exmoor. Penoyre (2005, 15) notes that walls made of this material are often so rough as to need rendering in lime mortar. However, no significant trace of lime wall facing was found at Longforth Farm and it is possible that the wall facing was not rendered.

A 'skim' of lime render was recorded in a small section of the drain passing through the base of the garderobe, and this may suggest that in this area at least the stonework was pargeted or 'lined' out in order to stop water and effluent penetrating the core of the walling.

Remarkably perhaps, not a single fragment of door, window or other moulding was recovered, although this also might be attributed to the extensive later robbing of the building. Such mouldings may have been made of Ham Stone, an Upper Lias deposit quarried at Ham Hill to the east.

Roofing Slate
by Lorraine Mepham

Roofing slate was recovered in similar quantities to the ceramic ridge tiles (see below), although this assemblage constitutes a small sample (probably no more than 5%) of the quantities encountered on site, particularly from demolition deposits. The 171 fragments collected focused on the more complete examples.

The raw material falls into three groups: pale greyish or purplish slates, tending to lamination (type 1); pale greyish or greenish, very similar to type 1 (type 2); and harder, darker grey slates (type 3). The source(s) for the slates is assumed to lie somewhere in the south-west peninsula, probably in the slate beds of the Brendon Hills, where they were quarried at

Figure 4.1 Slate roof-tiles (numbers 1–9)

north Wiveliscombe and further west at Treborough (Penoyre 2005, 15).

Slates of types 1 and 2 are subrectangular, often with rounded 'shoulders', always longer than they are broad. Type 3 slates are generally markedly narrow. A number of slates of all types preserve surviving dimensions, widths and/or lengths, both from top to tail (bottom edge), and from peg hole to tail, which is the more important measurement (the slates were top-hung, and as such did not require a standard distance from peg-hole to head: Thorp 1996, 291). The lower edge ('tail') is generally neatly cut and straight. Peg holes are generally central, although one or two slates have off-centre peg holes. A few slates have two peg holes, perhaps due to the replacement of an original damaged hole. One slate has a slit instead of a rounded peg hole. The slates would presumably have been mortared in place once hung (*ibid.*, 291), but few clear traces of mortar were observed, and thus the slate-free 'margins' (which also related to the gauge of the pegged slates) could not be measured. The margin would have been the area of the tile exposed to the open air, the remainder covered by the slates in the course above; most historic pegslates from the medieval period through to the 19th century had a three-slate lap, sometimes increasing to four (*ibid.*, 292).

Of the 171 slates collected, 63 retained surviving original measurements, though in only 22 cases did this include both length and width (for the remainder only the width was measurable). This small sample gives insufficient data to comment on the possible grading of slate sizes in the same way as has been possible, for example, for Berry Pomeroy castle (Thorp 1996). For slates of types 1 and 2 (Fig. 4.1, 1–6), which were clearly related, lengths (13 measurable examples) range from 125 to 340 mm, with six examples falling within the range of 150–195 mm. Measurable widths (30 examples) range from 70–300 mm. These tiles have a wide range of sizes and, while they may well have conformed to the regional pattern of diminishing courses from bottom to top of the roof, specific graded sizes are not discernible here.

Tiles of type 3 (Fig. 4.1, 7–9) show a more restricted size range, being long and narrow. Measurable lengths (nine examples) range from 135–290 mm, and widths (33 examples) from 55–170 mm, with 18 falling within the range 80–110 mm. These are, on average, slightly thicker than the slates of types 1 and 2. This fact, together with the quite different colouring of these slates, suggests that they may not have been used together with types 1 and 2; there may be some chronological difference, but without well stratified deposits this cannot be determined.

Although it seems certain that the hall and other principal elements in the complex were roofed with stone, there is a reference of 1343 (see Chapter 2) to 'houses in the court need thatching'. If this does refer to the Longforth Farm site, then it indicates that at least some other buildings there did not have slate coverings.

Table 4.1 Ceramic building material by type

Type	Total No.
Floor tile (decorated)	59
Floor tile (plain)	44
Floor tile (undiagnostic, no surfaces)	15
Hearth/floor	78
Roof tile	567
Total	763

List of illustrated slates
Fig. 4.1
1. Slate, type 1. Context 602, roof collapse in Room 6
2. Slate, type 1. Context 602, roof collapse in Room 6
3. Slate, type 2. Context 602, roof collapse in Room 6
4. Slate, type 2. Context 602, roof collapse in Room 6
5. Slate, type 1. Context 824, pit 820 in Group 10060 (post-medieval spread)
6. Slate, type 1. Context 629, demolition layer
7. Slate, type 3. Context 962, demolition layer
8. Slate, type 3. Context 629, demolition layer
9. Slate, type 3. Context 725, demolition layer

Ceramic Building Material
by Lorraine Mepham

The assemblage of ceramic building material (CBM) amounts to 824 fragments, weighing 86,987 g. This includes fragments of floor tile, hearth/floor tile, brick and drainpipe, but the majority comprises fragments of glazed roof tile. CBM of post-medieval date (brick and drainpipe), which is likely to represent incidental finds rather than specifically relating to the structures excavated, has been omitted here, along with a small number of undiagnostic fragments. This leaves 763 fragments; Table 4.1 gives the quantification (by fragment count) by type.

Ridge Tiles

The majority of the CBM assemblage from Longforth comprises fragments of roof tile, and all of these appear to belong to glazed ridge tiles, including crested examples. No flat peg tiles were recovered, and it seems clear that the medieval buildings were roofed in slate, with ceramic tiles restricted to the ridges, a pattern commonly seen across the south-west, where there were plentiful supplies of slate suitable for roofing (see above).

The ridge tiles are U-profiled or V-profiled tiles, with applied, knife-cut crests (in some cases the crests have detached from the tiles). The sides of the crests are slashed, which would have acted as a decorative technique but would also have served to strengthen the crest/tile join and to prevent the tiles from misfiring in the kiln. There is some minor variation in the size and slashing of the crests (Fig. 4.2, 1–5). The tiles are glazed, although the glaze does not extend to the edges of the tiles and can be unevenly applied (see Pl. 7.2). The tiles are fired to a mid-red/pink colour, with some harder-fired (or over-fired) examples fired to a darker red; glaze appears yellow-green, or dark olive on harder-fired tiles.

A sample of the ridge tiles examined under the microscope, combined with macroscopic examination

33

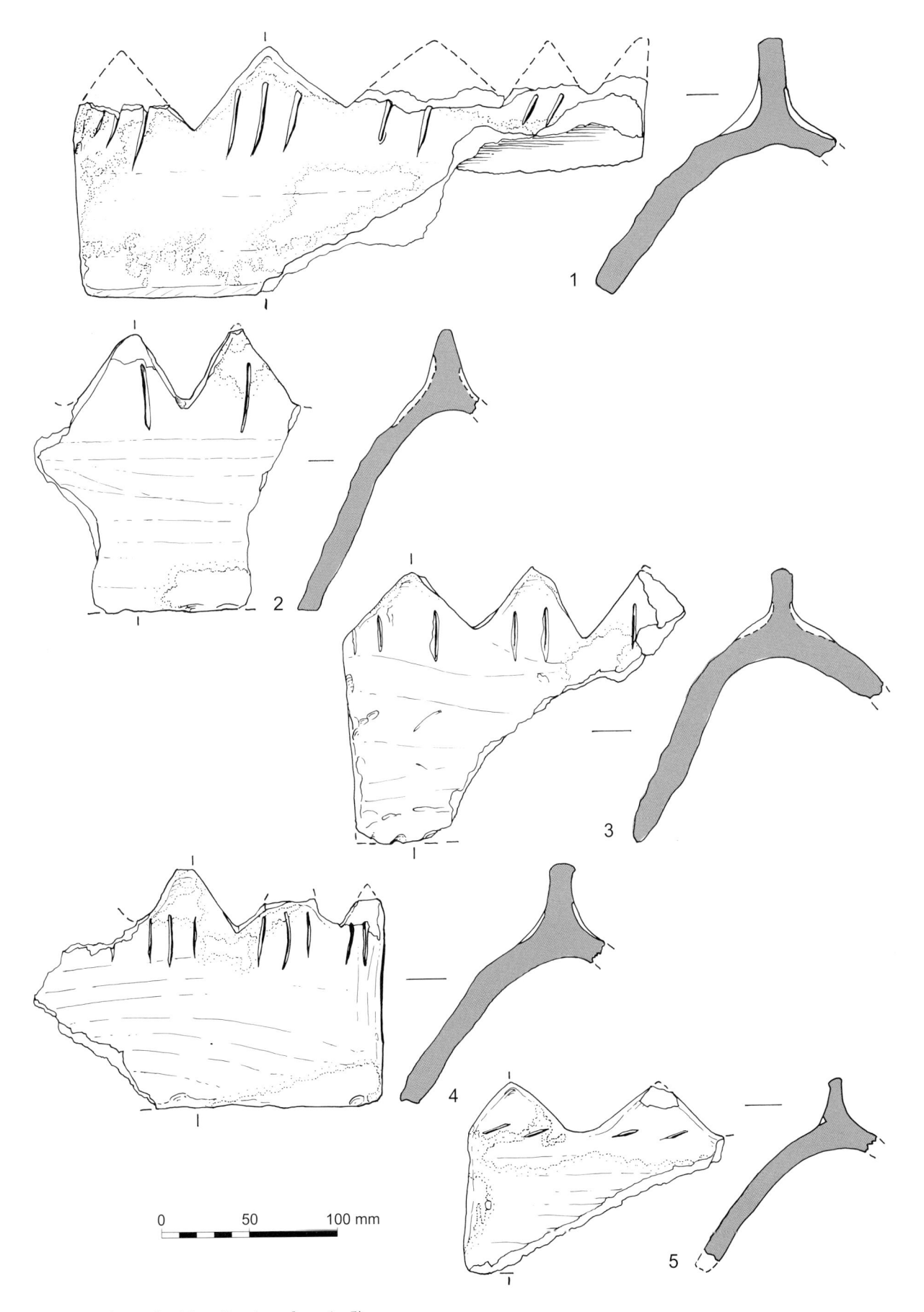

Figure 4.2 Ceramic ridge tiles (numbers 1–5)

of the remainder, suggests that the majority utilised a coarse fabric type, tending to lamination, and containing distinctive rock inclusions, including soft, shiny pinkish and greyish inclusions. These inclusions are also characteristic of Romano-British 'Norton Fitzwarren-type' pottery, which has a presumed source to the south-west of Taunton, around Norton Fitzwarren (Timby 1989, 54) – in other words, the majority of the ceramic ridge tiles used at Longforth Farm are likely to have had a local source. While it is possible that the roof tiles may have been made on site as a special commission on the initial construction of the building, it is more likely that, following the pattern observed, for example, across Wessex, the tiles were produced in an established tile-making centre, in which production would have been on a large scale (Hare 1991, 94). The presence of several tiles showing signs of firing faults need not contradict this theory, since these faults are not so severe as to render them unusable, making them 'seconds' rather than wasters (Fig. 4.2, 4, for example, has a broken crest, glazed over the break). A tilery based in or close to Taunton, for example, could have been supplying the town itself, and its hinterland. A much smaller proportion of tiles are in finer, sandy fabrics, and could represent later additions and/or repairs to the original roofs. These are broadly comparable to ridge tiles found in Taunton and dated to the 13th/14th century (Pearson 1984, pottery type 161, mf I.C1, II.C2, no. 753), and the tiles in coarse fabrics are likely to have a similar date range; they are certainly unlikely to pre-date the 13th century (Salzmann 1952, 229).

The largest groups of ridge tiles came from a roof collapse layer in Room 6 in the north range and from a general demolition layer across the building. Others were found in various layers across the site, but generally in post-abandonment contexts.

List of illustrated ridge tiles
Fig. 4.2
1. Ridge tile, fabric 1, complete length. Demolition layer 629
2. Ridge tile, fabric 1. Demolition layer 602
3. Ridge tile, fabric 1. Demolition layer 1294
4. Ridge tile, fabric 1. Demolition layer 602
5. Ridge tile, fabric 2. Demolition layer 629

Floor Tiles

Both decorated and plain tiles were used as flooring in the medieval building. None were found *in situ*, although one plain and eight decorated tiles were found in the area of Room 10, in the western part of the north range. Other tiles were found in demolition layers, robber trenches and other post-occupation deposits. The majority of the tiled pavement(s) is likely to have been deliberately stripped out, or robbed, soon after the building was abandoned.

Both plain and decorated tiles were made in similar fabrics, fine and silty with few visible inclusions apart from occasional red iron compounds; there is nothing distinctive about these fabrics and, in the absence of any widespread programme of petrological analysis, the full pattern of production and distribution of floor tiles in Somerset (as elsewhere) cannot be understood. No medieval tile kilns have yet been found in Somerset, although wasters have been found at Keynsham, Taunton and Glastonbury (Rodwell 2001, 449; Lowe 2003, 8).

Seven different designs were recorded from the decorated tiles (59 fragments, representing a maximum of 36 tiles, one of which is illegible) (Fig. 4.3, 1–8; see also Pl. 7.3). None are complete, and some designs are represented only by small fragments. Four of the designs are on square tiles, and all these conform to a single size: 140 mm, or 5½ inches square. Three designs are on rectangular tiles; two of these (designs 529 and 530, 'Richard and Saladin') are larger – 160 mm (6¼ inches) in depth, though the full width is unknown. The third rectangular tile is represented by a small corner fragment only (design 119), and its original size is unknown.

The plain tiles are in two forms, small square and rectangular. The square tiles (45 mm/1¾ inches square) are all glazed over a white slip, appearing yellow; while the rectangular tiles (140 mm/ 5½ inches x 45 mm/1¾ inches) have a dark, almost black glaze, although this might be due to wear – where the glaze appears fresher, it has a darkish green tint. These plain tiles were used in borders, presumably in conjunction with the decorated tiles, either around the edges of the floor(s) or, more probably, to delineate panels within the decorative design. Part of the tile pavement in the Corpus Christi chapel in Wells Cathedral uses the latter effect with very similar near-black and yellow border tiles, the four-tile panels bounded by dark rectangular tiles, with the yellow square tiles used at the intersections (Rodwell 2001, figs 464–5, carpet 4). Analysis of the Wells border tiles showed that they had been cut from tiles of standard sizes – in other words, the same forms were used in production of both decorated and plain tiles, as it would have been essential that the dimensions of each sort should correlate, otherwise layouts would have been compromised (*ibid*., 479). The Longforth tiles conform to this pattern, each 'standard' tile producing three rectangular tiles or nine small square tiles. The scoring (extending only about halfway through the tile thickness) is clearly visible on most of the tiles, and two rectangular tiles are still joined.

Figure 4.3 Ceramic floor tiles (number 1–8)

Parallels for all seven designs on the decorated tiles, at comparable sizes, were found amongst the published corpus of medieval tiles from Somerset (Lowe 2003); all are of the 'Wessex School', a description that relates to a series of designs derived initially from those on tiles laid in the Queen's Chamber at Clarendon Palace, Wiltshire, during 1250–2 (Eames 1988). The occurrence of the seven designs is summarised in Table 4.2. All seven have been recorded at Glastonbury Abbey, while individual designs have been found variously at Wells Cathedral (Rodwell 2001), Cleeve Abbey (Harcourt 2000), Old Cleeve Church and Bridgwater Friary (Lowe 2003).

Lowe dates six of the seven within the second half of the 13th century, with design 203 (quartered circle with fleurs-de-lis) spanning the 13th/14th century, but parallels with the Wells tile series suggests a slightly later date, at least for the square tiles. At the latter site, Drury argues that tiles of group 2 (which include four of the Longforth designs – see Table 4.2) mark a development of the initial Wessex School series, incorporating more naturalistic foliage motifs, and more heraldic designs. The development is paralleled at the tile kiln at Nash Hill in Wiltshire, and Drury suggests that the group 2 tiles found at Wells were made by a tiler moving from Nash Hill and possibly operating at Glastonbury towards the end of the 13th century; the workshop may still have been flourishing in the 1320s (Drury 2001, 458). The 'Richard and Saladin' tiles may be earlier. Tiles of this design were evidently made in an earlier phase of manufacture at Glastonbury, from dies represented at Clarendon Palace; Drury places these tiles in the early phase of the Wessex School, between the 1240s and 1260s (*ibid.*, 459). At Cleeve Abbey, where fabric

Table 4.2 *Decorated floor tile designs (design numbers follow Lowe 2003; Wells designs from Rodwell 2001)*

Design No.	Description	No. examples	Notes
119	Rectangular border tile; lion in circle flanked with foliate scrolls (Fig. 4.3, 1)	1	late 13th century
147	Two addorsed birds in circle (Fig. 4.3, 2)	6	late 13th century (Wells 52)
186	Foliated saltire with lis ends (Fig. 4.3, 3, 4)	10	late 13th century; one halved diagonally (triangular tile) (Wells 50)
203	Quarter circle across each corner containing vestigial fleur-de-lis (Fig. 4.3, 5)	3	13th/14th century (Wells 56)
478	Arms 'Chequy argent and sable' set diagonally (Fig. 4.3, 6)	12	third quarter 13th century (Wells 63)
529	rectangular tile; mounted knight (Richard) (Fig. 4.3, 7)	2	forms pair with design 530; mid–late 13th century
530	Rectangular tile; mounted knight (Saladin) (Fig. 4.3, 8)	1	forms pair with design 529; mid–late 13th century

analysis suggests a local source, they are dated to between 1244 and 1272 (Harcourt 2000, 47).

In the 13th and early 14th centuries, the manufacture of tiled pavements would have been expensive, confined to royal palaces, ecclesiastical buildings, and the houses of rich laymen. Initially at least, tiled pavements would have been special commissions, the tiles manufactured by itinerant craftsmen on or very close to the site (Drury 2001, 459; Lowe 2003, 2). Later in the 13th century, it is clear that the Nash Hill tilery in Wiltshire, established *c.* 1270, was supplying a wide area, tiles being sent as far as Wells; later, as we have seen, Nash Hill may have spawned a separate production centre at Glastonbury, supplying the south-west region. The pavement(s) at Longforth, therefore, may have been constructed using tiles made in Somerset, perhaps at Glastonbury, given the occurrence of all the Longforth designs there, but not necessarily by itinerant craftsmen working on the site itself. The occurrence of two rectangular border tiles still joined together is suggestive, but if, as has been suggested, plain and decorated tiles were supplied as a 'kit' (Drury 2001, 479), then the border tiles might have been supplied scored but unsplit.

The parallels with other sites in Somerset are all with ecclesiastical sites; there are no parallels, as far as is known, from any other secular sites, and the Longforth assemblage constitutes the largest known from a secular site in the county. Interestingly, the 'Richard and Saladin' tiles, possibly earlier in date, could indicate more than one period of tile use at Longforth. The use of the heraldic tiles (design 478; Wells design 63) could give some clue to the ownership of the building. These arms were borne by several families; Lowe links them to St Barbe, who owned lands in South Brent and Ashington (Lowe 2003, 51), while at Wells they are identified with de Warenne (Rodwell 2001, 475).

List of illustrated floor tiles
Fig. 4.3
1. Rectangular border tile; lion in circle flanked with foliate scrolls (Lowe design 119). Object Number (ON) 82, construction cut 839
2. Rectangular tile; two addorsed birds in circle (design 147). ON 16, unstratified
3. Rectangular tile; foliated saltire with lis ends (design 186). ON 52, demolition layer 1333
4. Triangular tile, split from rectangular design (design 186). ON 75, layer 329
5. Rectangular tile; quarter circle across each corner containing vestigial fleur-de-lis (design 203). ON 14, unstratified
6. Rectangular tile; arms 'Chequy argent and sable', set diagonally (design 478). ON 41, demolition layer 1183
7. Rectangular tile; mounted knight (Richard) (design 529). ON 45, demolition layer 1185
8. Rectangular tile; mounted knight (Saladin) (design 530). ON 76, demolition layer 629

Floor/Hearth Tiles

A number of fragments (78) are in a very coarse, friable fabric containing prominent quartz grains, and derive from square tiles ranging from 30 to 45 mm in thickness. Although these coarse tiles have the appearance of hearth tiles, they lack the usual stabbed holes that characterise these forms, and in some cases the upper surface is worn smooth. It seems that they were probably used as floor tiles, possibly in the service areas of the building complex.

Chapter 5
Finds

Pottery
by Lorraine Mepham

The pottery assemblage amounts to 959 sherds (11,618 g), and includes material of prehistoric, Romano-British, medieval and post-medieval date, with a clear focus in the medieval period. The condition of the material is fair to good; the assemblage is highly fragmented, but levels of surface and edge abrasion are generally low, probably due at least in part to the hard-fired nature of the medieval and post-medieval fabrics. Mean sherd weight overall is 12.1 g; when broken down this drops to 11.8 g for the medieval assemblage, and rises again to 21.6 g for the post-medieval assemblage. For prehistoric and Romano-British pottery the mean weight is significantly less (9.1 g and 5.5 g respectively).

The prehistoric and medieval pottery has been subjected to full fabric and form analysis, following the standard Wessex Archaeology pottery recording system (Morris 1994), which accords with national guidelines (Medieval Pottery Research Group (MPRG) 2001; Prehistoric Ceramics Research Group (PCRG) 2010). Vessel forms have been defined following nationally recommended nomenclature (MPRG 1998).

Prehistoric and Romano-British

Prehistoric pottery amounts to 130 sherds (1180 g), which is largely made up of a single group of 107 sherds from one context in Area B (gully 10017). This group of sherds appear to represent a single vessel, in a coarse grog-tempered fabric (a single medieval sherd from the same context can be regarded as intrusive). The vessel is in poor condition, with worn edges and abraded surfaces. A few body sherds carry twisted cord impressed decoration (Fig. 5.1, 2), but the overall design is unknown. One sherd comes from the rim of the vessel (Fig. 5.1, 1), and suggests an upright flat-topped rim. On the grounds of form, fabric and decoration, an attribution to the Trevisker style of the Early/Middle Bronze Age is most likely, and the rim form would place this vessel within Parker Pearson's functional classification as Style 2 (Parker Pearson 1990). These are bucket-shaped vessels with decoration below the rim, and usually with a series of lugs around a slight shoulder, possibly smaller storage or cooking vessels. Grog-tempering was commonly used for Trevisker ceramics in Somerset (Parker Pearson 1995, 97). Quinnell, in her recent review of Trevisker ceramics, illustrates two such vessels from a barrow just north of Exeter, also in grog-tempered fabrics, and with similar impressed cord decoration (Quinnell 2012, fig. 4). Grog-tempered Trevisker-related vessels with similar decoration have been recorded from Norton Fitzwarren (Woodward 1989, fig. 18), and from a recently excavated site at Queen Camel (Wessex Archaeology 2016). Trevisker ceramics from Somerset seem to be confined to the Middle Bronze Age, in contrast to the longer, Early to Middle Bronze Age date range seen in Devon and Cornwall (Quinnell 2012, 164–5).

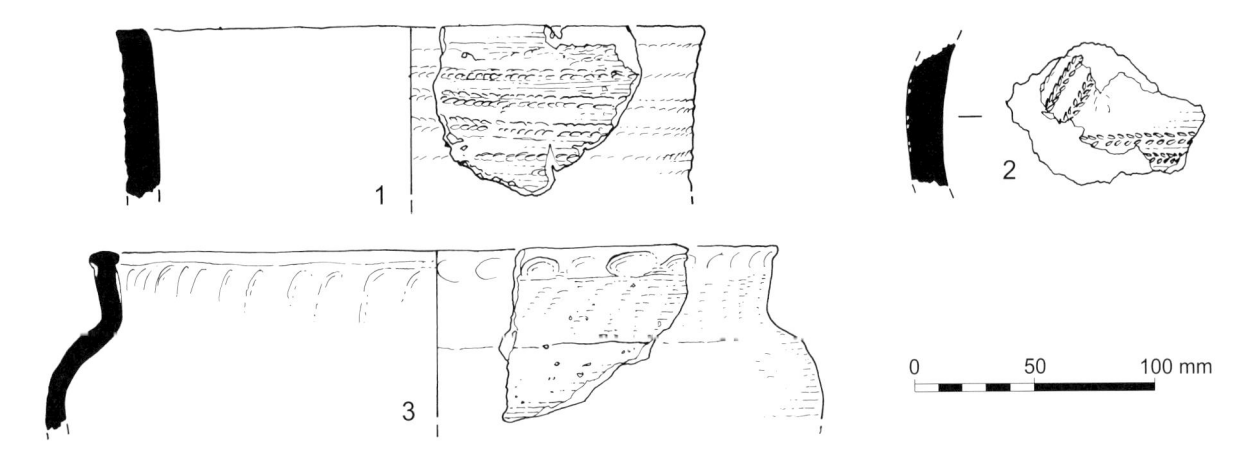

Figure 5.1 Prehistoric pottery (numbers 1–3)

Two grog-tempered sherds from gully 10014 in Area D, one from gully 10116 in Area B (possibly part of the medieval enclosure system), and two from ditch 352 in Area A, all small, undiagnostic body sherds, are also tentatively dated as Bronze Age on fabric grounds, and could also belong to the Trevisker ceramic tradition.

Thirteen sherds in flint-tempered fabrics (all from erosion gully 10002), and five sandy sherds (four found residually in medieval pit 380 and one from post-medieval ditch 106) are broadly dated as late prehistoric (Late Bronze Age to Middle Iron Age). The only diagnostic pieces are the four sherds from pit 380, which form the rim of a shouldered vessel of probable Early Iron Age date (Fig. 5.1, 3).

There is a smattering of Romano-British sherds (12 sherds; 66 g), comprising coarse sandy wares, with two sherds of samian and one of Oxfordshire colour-coated fineware. All sherds are abraded and all were either demonstrably or almost certainly residual in the contexts in which they were found.

Medieval

Medieval wares make up the bulk of the pottery assemblage (745 sherds; 8817 g) (Table 5.1). These fall into several groups, based on dominant inclusion type, and these are described below.

Table 5.1 Medieval and post-medieval pottery fabric totals

Fabric Code	Description	No. sherds	Wt (g)
L400	Soft fired, slightly micaceous, calcareous fabric; moderate voids, rounded or irregular, <3 mm	2	10
Q400	Hard, coarse fabric with prominent inclusions (<3 mm): rounded quartz with some subangular quartzite and other rock inclusions	350	3073
Q401	Hard, sandy fabric; well sorted, subrounded quartz <0.25 mm, mostly iron-stained; some examples have rare subangular quartzite <2 mm	69	699
Q402	Hard, sandy fabric; relatively well sorted subangular/ subrounded quartz <0.5 mm; sparse sandstone and other rock inclusions <0.1mm	59	526
Q403	Hard fabric; common, fairly well sorted, subrounded quartz (iron-stained) <1 mm; slightly micaceous	5	59
Q404	Hard, sandy fabric; common, well sorted quartz <0.25 mm; often glazed; as fabric Q407 but reduced	2	5
Q405	Hard, slightly micaceous fabric containing common fine sand; rare soft grey inclusions; generally oxidised with unoxidised core and/or internal surface	63	1076
Q406	Hard fabric; common, well sorted glauconitic quartz <0.25 mm; generally reduced with oxidised surface(s); glazed	38	622
Q407	Medium-grained glazed ware (well sorted quartz <0.25 mm), oxidised	21	331
Q408	Hard white-firing fabric; sparse, well sorted, subangular/ subrounded quartz <0.5 mm; slightly gritty feel; generally glazed	6	52
Q409	Very hard-fired, dense matrix containing moderate fine sand; unoxidised, glazed	20	542
R400	Hard fabric containing moderate, poorly sorted, subangular/ subrounded quartz <0.5 mm; sparse to moderate, poorly sorted subangular rock fragments <3 mm (soft, silvery-grey and pinkish)	40	968
R401	Hard fabric, slightly soapy feel; sparse quartzite <1 mm and rock (sandstone?) inclusions <2 mm	68	825
E521	Saintonge	2	29
	Sub-total medieval	745	8817
E485	'Tudor Green'	6	118
E600	Redware	49	1216
E672	Martincamp flask	1	27
E695	Staffs-/Bristol-type slipware	6	118
E740	Refined whiteware	6	59
E750	Creamware	1	1
E790	English stoneware	1	4
E805	Bone china	1	3
E830	Porcelain	1	9
	Sub-total post-medieval	72	1555
	Total	817	10,372

Group 1: Upper Greensand-derived wares (fabric Q400)

These wares make up 35% of the total medieval assemblage by weight, and are characterised by the inclusions of polished quartz and chert. They are found almost exclusively in jar forms (32 examples) in various sizes (rim diameters range from 240 mm to 340 mm). The jars have undeveloped rims (everted, with rim profiles thickened and generally internally bevelled; Fig. 5.2, 1, 2); one is finger impressed. There are also two jug rims, one with a pulled lip (Fig. 5.2, 4), and one with a strap handle stump; and a second jug handle, which is the only glazed sherd amongst these coarsewares. There is also part of a pedestal lamp, with a transverse pre-firing perforation through the pedestal (Fig. 5.2, 9).

This ware tradition is now well known in Somerset and the surrounding region, and petrological work has indicated a source (or rather, a series of sources) in the Blackdown Hills south of Taunton (Allan 2003). Examples of Upper Greensand-derived wares (sometimes described as 'chert-tempered') have been identified in Taunton (Pearson 1984, pottery type 55; Allan *et al.* 2010) and Exeter (Allan 1984, fabric 20), and the date range extends from the 10th to the 14th centuries. Internally bevelled rims are seen in Exeter from the earliest groups, possibly late 10th century until the late 13th century or later (*ibid.*, 4, fig. 3, rim types U and X); there are also a few examples here of the 'cupped' rim profile which makes its appearance *c.* 1200 (*ibid.* 4, rim type T). A date range of 11th to 13th century is suggested here; sherds were found in one feature which appeared to pre-date the medieval building (ditch 10055), but were also found in the enclosure ditches and pits to the east, whose use is presumed to be contemporaneous with the building.

Group 2: Sandy coarsewares (fabrics Q401, Q402, Q403)

The sandy wares, which make up 15% of the medieval total by weight, share some characteristics, but do not necessarily represent a single source or source area. Fabric Q401 contains well-sorted, fine quartz as well as occasional chert; fabric Q403 contains well sorted, coarse, rounded quartz; and fabric Q402 contains more subangular quartz and occasional greensand inclusions.

The sandy wares are also used almost exclusively for jars (11 examples), with similar undeveloped rim forms, although there are some with more developed profiles; two jar rims have 'cupped' profiles. The only other vessel form represented is a costrel in fabric Q402 (Fig. 5.2, 8), sherds of which were found in ditch 10095, to the east of the service range. The costrel is barrel-shaped, with one flat end and one rounded end; it has a centrally placed mouth between paired, pierced lug handles on the shoulders. It is patchily glazed over crudely applied, slip-painted decoration. Only two other sherds in this group of fabrics are glazed, and there is no other evidence of decoration.

Broad parallels can be found in Taunton (Pearson 1984), and the date range is likely to be similar to that of the greensand-derived wares, ie, 11th to 13th century, although fabric Q401 is likely to fall later in that range rather than earlier, say 12th to 13th century, and the costrel in Q402 is no earlier than late 13th century, and possibly 14th century (see below). There are documentary references to medieval pottery production in the later 13th century at Milverton, to the north of Wellington, and at Wellington itself (Le Patourel 1968, table III, fig. 25; Pearson 1984, fig. 57).

Group 3: Rock-tempered wares (R400, R401)

These wares (20% of the total by weight) are linked only by their use of rock inclusions. Fabric R400, represented largely by sherds of a single vessel (Fig. 5.2, 3), contains soft, pale silvery-grey and pinkish inclusions, which are identical to the inclusions found in Romano-British pottery in the area (although these sherds are certainly medieval); this Romano-British type has been linked to production at Norton Fitzwarren (Timby 1989; Holbrook and Bidwell 1991, 175, fabric 107). The date of the vessel, a jar from an ambiguous feature (10081) in Room 3 of the north range, falls within the range of 11th to 13th century.

Fabric R401 has a slightly soapy texture, and contains mixed inclusions, including quartzite and possible sandstone fragments. Diagnostic vessel forms comprise seven jars, with both undeveloped and developed rims, and two jugs, one with a pulled lip (Fig. 5.2, 5), and one with a strap handle. A date range of 11th to 13th century is again suggested.

Group 4: Calcareous wares (L400)

This group is represented by two sherds, both from the same context and undoubtedly from the same vessel. The fabric is heavily leached, with irregular voids, assumed to have originally contained calcareous inclusions. The source is uncertain, but there are Lias outcrops to the south of Taunton.

Group 5: Finer sandy wares (Q404–Q409)

The fine wares (30% of the total by weight) are generally glazed, and appear to derive mainly from jug forms (Fig. 5.2, 6, 7); some of these wares are white-slipped under a green glaze, while others carry painted slip decoration beneath the glaze. There is one costrel in fabric Q409 (the only vessel in this fabric from the site), from the same ditch as the example in fabric Q402 (Pl. 5.1). This costrel is cylindrical; it has one flat end, while the other is missing, but the central mouth and paired pierced

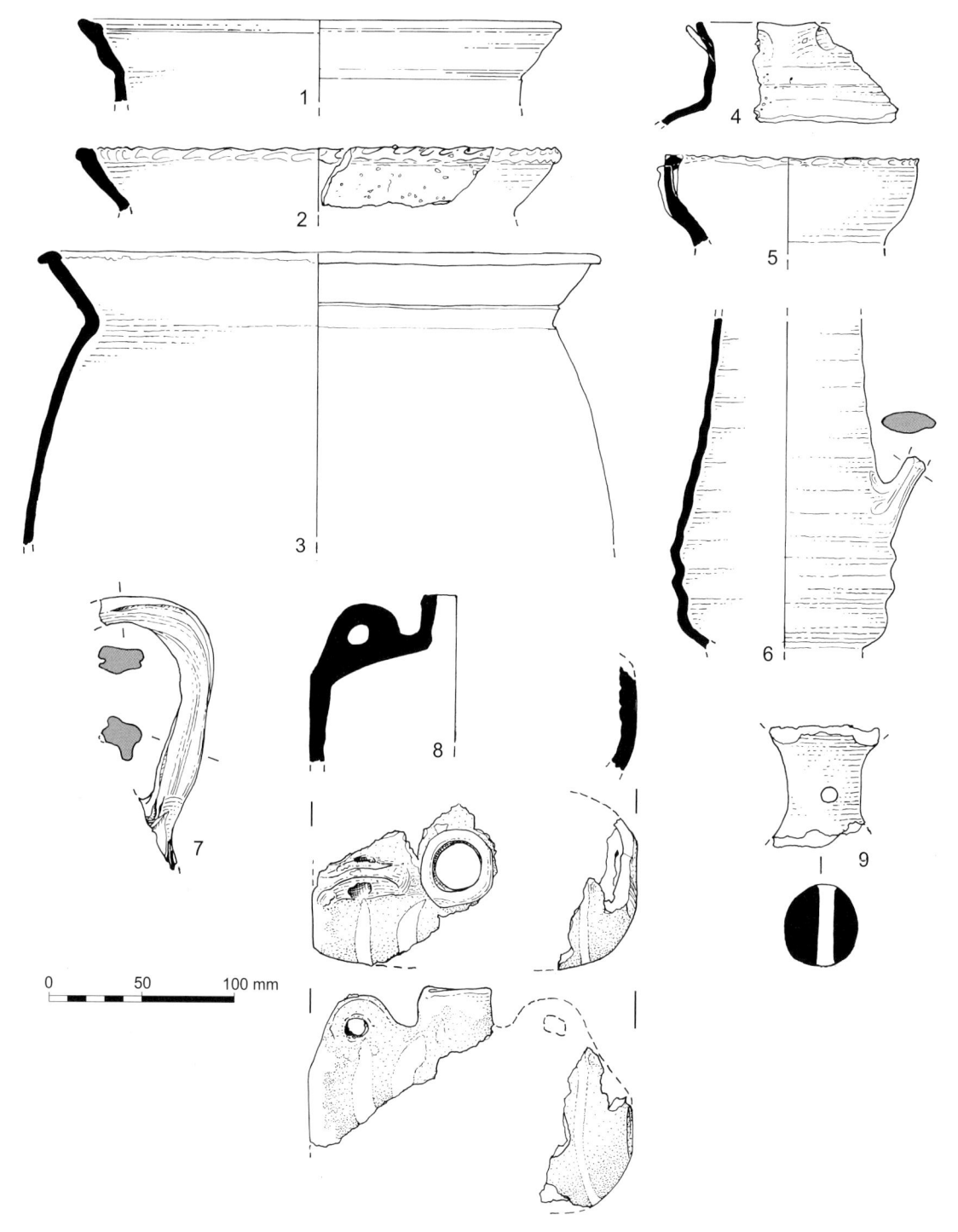

Figure 5.2 Medieval pottery (numbers 1–9)

lugs echo the barrel-shaped costrel in Q402. These vessels would have been used to store and transport liquids, suspended from a belt or strap by means of the pierced lugs. Dunning, in his early survey of barrel-shaped and cylindrical costrels dates their introduction in England, probably from northern France, to the late 13th century, and found their distribution restricted to the southern part of the country (Dunning 1964). There is no reason to amend Dunning's dating and, although the distribution of these vessels is now likely to be wider and more numerous, this is still an uncommon type – there are no examples, for instance, illustrated amongst the large published assemblage from Taunton (Pearson 1984).

Some of these sandy wares (eg, Q405, Q406) are likely to fall within the 'south Somerset' ceramic tradition, as exemplified by the products of the Donyatt production centre (Coleman-Smith and Pearson 1988). These have a potential date range of

Plate 5.1 Costrel (fabric Q409) from ditch 10095

14th to 16th centuries. Other slightly coarser fabrics (Q404, Q407, and the whiteware Q408) are dated slightly earlier, 13th to 14th century.

Group 6: Imports
These are limited to two sherds of Saintonge ware, both found in Area B. One is a body sherd with polychrome decoration and a thin lead glaze (from a demolition layer), while the second is a jug handle in an unglazed whiteware, possibly also from a polychrome vessel (from a robber trench). Saintonge polychrome has a date range of late 13th to early 14th century; it is commonly found in major south coast ports such as Plymouth and Exeter, but inland its occurrence seems to be restricted to higher status sites, for example manorial and religious.

Post-medieval

The post-medieval assemblage is small (Table 5.1). The most common ware types are coarse redwares, both glazed and unglazed. These mark a development of the late medieval fine sandy wares (and are likely in some cases to derive from the same south Somerset source(s)); in some cases the distinction between the two types is not easily determined. Redwares are used for utilitarian forms, here seen mainly as jugs and bowls. A 16th/17th-century date range can be suggested for these, although the presence of a few slipwares (both trailed slip and sgraffito techniques) could push them into the 18th century.

Six sherds of 'Tudor Green' ware from the Surrey/Hampshire border industry, dated as late 14th to late 15th or early 16th century, all from a demolition layer in Area B, overlap in date range with the medieval fine sandy wares (see above), and could represent the latest wares associated with the occupation of the building complex.

Part of an imported Martincamp flask (from a robber cut in the north range of the building) is of a type common in the 17th century (Hurst *et al.* 1986, 103–4, type III), a few sherds of Staffordshire-/Bristol-type marbled slipwares date from the later 17th to 18th centuries, and one sherd of English dipped stoneware and one of white salt glaze to the first half of the 18th century. Later factory-produced refined wares are notable by their scarcity (eight sherds).

Discussion

Chronology
The chronological focus of the assemblage lies in the medieval period, and the provenance here is significant: these finds are associated with the construction and occupation of a substantial and presumably high status building complex, probably manorial. The assemblage thus immediately assumes a significance by virtue of belonging to a type of site (medieval high status rural settlement) which is rarely represented in the region.

There are, however, limitations in the evidence. The relatively low proportion of domestic refuse is notable; it seems that this was disposed of elsewhere, outside the excavated area. There are no large pit groups, or midden deposits; amongst the pottery assemblage, for example, there are only eight feature groups of 25 sherds or greater, and the highest total per feature was 35 sherds; three of the eight features are likely to represent single-vessel sherd groups. This, combined with the predominance within the assemblage of coarsewares in a limited range of vessel forms which are not susceptible to close dating, limits the potential of the assemblage to provide a detailed chronological framework for the site.

Not even the construction date for the building complex can be confidently proposed. One feature, ditch 10055, appears to pre-date the medieval building complex in Area B, located beneath the solar block. This ditch contained 12 sherds, all in the greensand-derived fabric Q400, and including one finger-impressed jar rim of 11th- to 13th-century date (Fig. 5.2, 2). One other feature is more ambivalent – this is an amorphous, shallow feature on the northern edge of Room 3, which has an uncertain relationship with wall 10079 (it was cut by the later robber trench). Feature 10081 is either a tree-throw hole or, more probably, a shallow hollow in which material has accumulated. It contained 26 sherds, apparently all from a single jar (Fig. 5.2, 3). The relatively unabraded nature of the sherds suggests that they were deposited and buried relatively quickly, but whether this event took place prior to the building's construction, or during its use, remains unknown. The jar has only a broad date range of 11th to 13th century, so could belong to either phase.

Pottery from contexts within the building itself is very scarce, and is more likely to represent, for example, incidental sherds incorporated in construction cuts (and later robber cuts) rather than material directly associated with the occupation of the buildings. The latter is perhaps more likely to be seen in the sherds found in the ditches and pits of the enclosures to the east of the buildings. The enclosures appear to fall into two phases. Ditches and pits within the eastern group (and also the pits found in the western group) contained only coarsewares of 11th- to 13th-century date, while the ditches of the western group contained finer sandy wares of 13th century date and later. It may be the case, of course, that the pits and the eastern enclosures also pre-date the building complex; they share an alignment with the buildings, but also with the early ditch 10055. A connection with the buildings, however, seems more likely.

Later medieval pottery (14th century and later) was also found in contexts around the service range on the eastern side, confirming that this range did form a later addition to the complex.

As for when the buildings were abandoned, this presumably lies somewhere within the late medieval period, and the few sherds of 'Tudor Green' ware (late 14th to late 15th/early 16th century) could belong to this latest phase. Alternatively, and perhaps more probably, as they came only from one demolition layer, they could mark the beginning of the dismantling of the buildings.

Social Status

Pottery is not necessarily a good indicator of social status, as a cheap, easily accessible commodity. Nevertheless, there are certain broad trends that can be used. First, in rural areas, the proportion of glazed wares tends to be higher on sites higher up the social scale, for example manorial and religious sites. Second, these sites are more likely to have had access to imported wares. In this instance, the evidence is scanty. The two costrels, as uncommon forms, are of interest, but in general glazed wares seem to have been scarce on the site prior to the 14th century, and their occurrence in the late medieval period is in line with a general increase in glazed wares across the country, as the coarse kitchen wares were replaced by metal cooking vessels. Imports are limited to two sherds. Status in this case is more visible in the materials used to construct and adorn the building itself, such as the decorated floor tiles and glazed roof tiles.

List of illustrated vessels

Fig. 5.1
1. Trevisker vessel; rim; impressed twisted cord decoration; grog-tempered fabric. Context 316, gully 10017
2. Trevisker vessel; body sherd (same vessel as No. 1); grog-tempered fabric. Context 316, gully 10017
3. Late prehistoric shouldered jar; sandy fabric. Context 381, pit 380

Fig. 5.2
1. Jar rim; fabric Q400. Context 503, pit 10027
2. Jar rim; finger impressed decoration; fabric Q400. Context 706, ditch 10055
3. Jar profile; fabric R400. Context 838, hollow 10081
4. Jug rim; finger impressed decoration; pulled lip; fabric R401. Demolition layer 725
5. Jug rim, pulled lip; fabric Q400. Context 277, ditch 276
6. Jug, pear-shaped, with corrugated profile; base of strap handle; fabric Q4071. Context 899, gully terminal 898
7. Twisted jug handle; fabric Q405. Layer 102
8. Barrel costrel; one flat and one rounded end; pierced lug either side of neck. Painted slip decoration; partial glaze; fabric Q402. Context 1476/1562, ditch 10095
9. Pedestal lamp; pre-firing transverse perforation through pedestal; fabric Q400. Context 796, ditch 795

Worked and Burnt Flint
by Matt Leivers

Only 39 pieces of worked flint and chert were recovered. Much of this was undiagnostic flake debitage, but among the more diagnostic pieces at least four chronological periods are represented.

A single large blade from the subsoil is likely to date to the Terminal Upper Palaeolithic (Pl. 3.2). The piece is made on Greensand chert and measures 139 mm long by 39 mm wide. The butt is facetted. There is no crushing or bruising on the edges or dorsal ridges, but nevertheless the piece appears to belong to a Long Blade tradition. It is in very good condition.

Mesolithic blades, broken blades, blade and bladelet cores, as well as the distal portion of a lateral truncation and a serrated blade were found in various contexts, the majority from possible erosion channel 10002 in Area A, the source also of an end scraper of Late Neolithic type. Two scrapers made on thick irregular flakes are characteristic of rather less formal Early Bronze Age industries.

Although limited in numbers, the Terminal Upper Palaeolithic and Mesolithic material is of added significance due to the fact that no comparable material for the Terminal Palaeolithic and very little from the Mesolithic is known from the surrounding area. With the exception of a single blade from Pendine, Cornwall and a group from Solfach, Gwynedd, the Long Blade from Longforth Farm is the western-most example from Britain recorded to date. Mesolithic material in the area is scarce, limited to a single core and microlith from Milverton and a tranchet axe from Taunton (Wessex Archaeology and Jacobi 2014).

A very small quantity of burnt, unworked flint was present. This material type is intrinsically undatable, although often taken as an indicator of prehistoric activity. In this instance, the largest deposit (828 g) was associated with Early/Middle Bronze Age pottery in gully 10017. Other deposits (all very small) came from undated, medieval and post-medieval contexts.

Table 5.2 Other finds by material type

Material Type		No.	Wt (g)
Wall plaster		5	139
Fired clay		34	422
Stone		2	177
Glass		8	377
Clay pipe		13	47
Slag		20	3599
Metalwork		38	–
	Copper Alloy	1	–
	Lead	3	–
	Iron	34	–

Other Finds
by Lorraine Mepham

The very small quantities of other finds recovered are summarised in Table 5.2. Little of this material can be definitively attributed to the construction or occupation of the medieval buildings, most finds being recovered from post-abandonment deposits, and datable finds (vessel and window glass, clay tobacco pipe) are all post-medieval.

Structural materials, apart from the ceramic and stone roofing materials (see Chapter 4), are represented by wall plaster (monochrome white) and iron objects (nails, U-staple and looped fitting), some from medieval contexts.

A limited amount of functional evidence, possibly medieval, is provided by the ironworking slag. The largest fragment, from field system ditch 10003, appears to represent iron smelting, and the other fragments, although smaller and more abraded, could also be from smelting. The date of this material is uncertain, but the fragment from ditch 10109 was associated with a small group of medieval pottery. A lead weight, undatable, was recovered from a demolition layer, and there are two possible whetstones, also from demolition layers.

Chapter 6
Environment and Economy

Animal Bone
by L. Higbee

Only a small assemblage of animal bone was recovered, amounting to 378 fragments (2.132 kg). Once conjoins are taken into account this falls to 175 fragments. Only the medieval material is considered here.

Preservation

Bone preservation is on the whole quite good and most fragments show little or no sign of physical weathering. Cortical surfaces are intact and surface details such fine knife cuts are clear and easily observed. Poorly preserved fragments of bone were recovered from a few later medieval or post-medieval contexts, notably robber trenches, and these are assumed to have been reworked and re-deposited from earlier contexts.

Only two gnawed bones were noted in the whole assemblage. This is an extremely low incidence and suggests that scavenging dogs did not have open access to bone waste. It is also possible that the site was kept relatively clean and tidy, and any surface detritus was removed or buried before it could accumulate.

Medieval Material

Animal bone was recovered from 23 separate contexts of medieval date. The small assemblage includes the following species, which are listed in terms of their relative abundance: cattle, domestic fowl, sheep/goat, cod, horse and goose. Cattle and sheep/goat are both represented by cranial fragments and post-cranial bones, which suggests that livestock were brought to the site on the hoof where they were slaughtered, butchered and consumed. Age information is limited, however there is some suggestion that cattle were primarily kept for secondary products, in particular milk, and that pregnant ewes were kept on or close to the site during the lambing season.

The domestic fowl bones include elements from the wing and leg of a juvenile cockerel and an adult hen, whilst goose is represented by a fragment of distal ulna. The cod (*Gadus morhua*) bones comprise elements from the head including the dentary and maxilla.

During the processing of bulk soil samples for the recovery of charred plant remains, small animal bones were noted and recorded in the flots of two samples. In particular, large numbers of fish bones, including vertebrae, scales and otic bullae, were present in the sample from gully 1471.

Overall, however, there is nothing amongst this small assemblage of animal bone which might be indicative of a high status site.

Marine Shell
by Sarah F. Wyles

The marine shell augments the dietary evidence of the animal bone. Apart from one whelk, all of the shell recovered is oyster, and this includes both right and left valves, representing both preparation and consumption waste, but the quantities involved (23 shells) are very small. Either seafood did not form a major part of the medieval diet or (more likely) the waste was disposed of elsewhere outside the excavated area.

Charred Plant Remains
by Sarah F. Wyles

A total of 39 bulk samples from a range of features mainly of medieval date were processed for the recovery of charred plant remains and wood charcoal. As a result of their assessment a selection of eight samples from medieval features in Area B was made for further analysis of the charred plant assemblages. The selected samples were from the north range of the building complex, the south range, part of the enclosure system and various pits and postholes within this system.

Methods

The bulk samples for charred remains were generally of 20 litres and were processed by standard flotation methods; the flot retained on a 0.5 mm mesh, residues fractionated into 5.6 mm, 2 mm and

1 mm fractions. The coarse fractions (>5.6 mm) were sorted for artefacts and ecofacts, weighed and discarded.

At the analysis stage, all identifiable charred plant macrofossils were extracted from the flots, together with the 2 mm and 1 mm residues. Identification was undertaken using stereo incident light at magnifications of up to x40 using a Leica MS5 microscope, following the nomenclature of Stace (1997) for wild species and the traditional nomenclature as provided by Zohary and Hopf (2000, tables 3–5, 28, 65) for cereals, and with reference to modern reference collections where appropriate. The material identified was quantified and the results tabulated in Table 6.1.

Results

North range

The large assemblage recovered from layer 725 in Room 6 was dominated by grain fragments, in particular those of free-threshing wheat (*Triticum turgidum/aestivum* type). There were also a few free-threshing wheat rachis fragments and grains of rye (*Secale cereale*). The weed seed assemblage was dominated by those species typical of grassland, field margins and arable environments. These included seeds of vetch/wild pea (*Vicia/Lathyrus* sp.), oat/brome grass (*Avena/Bromus* sp.), brassica (*Brassica* sp.) and docks (*Rumex* sp.). There were also a few fragments of hazelnut (*Corylus avellana*) shell.

South range

The two assemblages analysed from the south range, from layer 690 in Room 10 and construction cut 10041, contained high numbers of charred remains. Again the cereal remains were predominant, particularly those of free-threshing wheat. There were also a small number of grains of barley (*Hordeum vulgare*) and grain and glume base fragments of hulled wheat, emmer or spelt (*Triticum dicoccum/spelta*). There was a single coleoptile recovered from layer 690.

Other possible crop remains included those of celtic bean (*Vicia faba*) and possible celtic bean/pea (*Vicia faba/Pisum sativium*). A number of the oats (*Avena* sp.) in the assemblages may also be of the cultivated variety. There were also a few fragments of hazelnut shell, a large number of sloe/hawthorn (*Prunus spinosa/Crataegus monogyna*) type thorns fragments and a charred alder (*Alnus* sp.) cone, indicative of the possible exploitation of a hedgerow/scrub environment and a wetter area.

The weed seed assemblages included seeds of vetch/wild pea, oat/brome grass, docks, stinking mayweed (*Anthemis cotula*) and red bartsia (*Odontites vernus*), and runch (*Raphanus raphanistrum*) capsules. Again the weed seed assemblages were dominated by those species typical of grassland, field margins and arable environments.

Enclosures

The sample from enclosure ditch 10034 produced almost equal numbers of cereal remains and weed seeds. Grain fragments outnumbered chaff elements, with those of free-threshing wheat being predominant. There were also remains of rye and barley. A single coleoptile fragment was recovered. Other possible crops were celtic bean/pea and oats. A few hazelnut shell fragments and a charred alder cone were noted.

The weed seeds included seeds of vetch/wild pea, oats/brome grass, docks, clover/medick (*Trifolium/Medicago* sp.), stinking mayweed and oxeye daisy (*Leucanthemum vulgare*). There were also a number of grass culm nodes.

Pit and posthole cluster

There are differences between the large assemblages in these analysed samples. Cereal remains are most numerous in the assemblage from pit 558, are present in almost equal numbers with weed seeds in pit 10025, and are outnumbered by weed seeds in posthole 534. There are more grain fragments than chaff elements in all three assemblages.

The cereal remains are mainly those of free-threshing wheat with some rye and barley present. Other possible crop remains included those of celtic bean and celtic bean/pea, with some of the oats also possibly being of the cultivated variety. A flax (*Linum usitatissimum*) seed was recovered from pit 10025 and triangular capsule fragments possibly of flax from pit 558.

The weed seed assemblages were dominated by seeds of vetch/wild pea, oat/brome grass and stinking mayweed, and included seeds of docks, sheep's sorrel (*Rumex acetosella* group), red bartsia, oxeye daisy, small scabious (*Scabiosa columbaria*) and cornflower (*Centaurea cyanus*), and runch capsules. Again, these species are typical of grassland, field margins and arable environments.

Other remains included hazelnut shell fragments, a few sloe/hawthorn thorn fragments and monocotyledon stem/root fragments.

Pit 633

A very rich plant assemblage of approximately 1400 items was recovered from pit 633. The weed seeds outnumbered the cereal remains. The cereal remains were predominantly those of free-threshing wheat with a relatively high number of those of rye and a few of those of barley and possibly hulled wheat. Although grain fragments are still more numerous,

Table 6.1 Charred plant remains from medieval features

Group		North range	South range		Enclosure ditch		Pit cluster		
Group Number				10041	10034	10025			
Feature type		Room 6 Layer	Room 2 Layer	Construction cut	Ditch	Pit	Pit	Posthole	Pit
Cut		–	–	972	550	562	558	534	633
Context		725	690	970	552	559	557	532	635
Vol (L)		30	20	20	20	10	10	9	20
Flot size		250	375	275	200	60	40	40	130
%Roots		35	15	2	25	50	15	25	20
Cereals	Common Name								
Hordeum vulgare L. sl (grain)	barley	–	2	2	1	–	3	1	1
Hordeum vulgare L. sl (rachis frag)	barley	–	–	–	1	3	6	3	6
Triticum dicoccum/spelta (grain)	emmer/spelt wheat	–	–	cf. 2	–	–	–	–	cf. 2
Triticum dicoccum/spelta (glume bases)	emmer/spelt wheat	–	1	–	–	–	–	–	–
Triticum turgidum/aestivum (grain)	free-threshing wheat	25	200	46	21	22	55	25	68
Triticum turgidum/aestivum (rachis frags)	free-threshing wheat	3	27	25	9	11	30	27	69
Secale cereale (grain)	rye	1	–	–	4	4	5	2	14
Secale cereale (rachis frag)	rye	–	–	–	cf. 4	cf. 3	cf. 8	1	cf. 13
Cereal indet. (grains)	cereal	42	125	100	90	70	130	90	225
Cereal frag. (est. whole grains)	cereal	26	75	45	10	10	25	35	50
Cereal frags (rachis frags)	cereal	–	1	–	26	30	39	18	167
Cereal frags (coleoptile)	cereal	–	1	–	1	–	–	–	–
Other Species									
Ranunculus sp.	buttercup	–	–	1	–	–	1	–	1
Alnus sp. (cone)	alder	–	–	1	1	–	–	–	–
Corylus avellana L. (fragments)	hazelnut	4 (<1 ml)	4 (<1 ml)	1 (<1 ml)	5 (<1 ml)	4 (<1 ml)	2 (<1 ml)	15 (1 ml)	5 (<1 ml)
Chenopodium sp.	goosefoot	–	1	2	2	–	–	1	–
Atriplex sp. L.	oraches	–	1	–	1	–	–	1	–
Stellaria sp. L.	stitchwort	–	–	–	–	–	–	1	–
Polygonum aviculare L.	knotgrass	–	1	–	3	–	–	–	–
Fallopia convolvulus (L.) À. Löve	black-bindweed	–	–	–	1	–	–	–	–
Rumex sp. L.	docks	3	4	3	6	5	8	9	6
Rumex acetosella group Raf.	sheep's sorrel	–	–	–	–	–	5	6	–

		7	3	3 7 frags	5	2 5 frags	5 2 capsules + 2 frags 3	3 1 capsule + 6 frags	15 4 capsules + 3 frags
Brassica sp. L.	brassica	–	–	–	–	–	–	–	1
Raphanus raphanistrum L.	runch	–	–	–	–	–	–	–	–
Prunus spinosa/Crataegus monogyna (thorns/twigs)	sloe/hawthorn type thorns	–	37	30	2	–	3	–	–
Vicia L./*Lathyrus* sp. L.	vetch/wild pea	22	76	25	41	25	65	68	535
Vicia faba L.	celtic bean	–	3	2	–	1	–	1	1
Vicia faba/Pisum sativium L.	celtic bean/pea	–	–	2	1	–	–	1	8
Lathyrus cf. *nissolia* L.	grass vetchling	–	–	–	–	–	1	–	–
Pisum sativium L.	pea	–	–	3	–	–	–	–	–
Medicago/Trifolium sp. L.	medick/clover	–	1	3	6	1	–	3	1
Linum usitatissimum L.	flax	–	–	–	–	–	1	–	–
Myosotis L.	forget-me-nots	–	1	–	–	–	–	–	–
Plantago lanceolata L.	ribwort plantain	–	–	–	1	–	–	–	–
Odontites vernus	red bartsia	–	–	2	–	1	–	–	–
Galium sp. L.	bedstraw	1	1	1	–	–	–	–	–
Valerianella dentata (L.) Pollich	narrow-fruited cornsalad	–	–	–	–	–	–	–	1
Scabiosa columbaria L.	small scabious	–	–	1	–	1	–	–	–
Centaurea cyanus L.	cornflower	–	–	–	3	–	3	1	9
Anthemis cotula L. (seeds)	stinking mayweed	–	1	6	3	14	8	10	11
Anthemis cotula L. (seed head)	stinking mayweed	–	–	–	–	–	–	–	2
Leucanthemum vulgare Lam.	oxeye daisy	–	–	–	3	8	8	4	3
Poaceae culm node	grass	–	–	–	8	1	–	–	13
Lolium/Festuca sp.	rye-grass/fescue	–	–	1	1	1	1	2	–
Poa/Phleum sp. L.	meadow grass/cat's-tails	1	1	1	1	–	–	–	–
Avena sp. L. (grain)	oat grain	–	21	9	10	10	7	36	15
Avena sp. L. (floret base)	oat floret	–	–	–	–	–	–	–	2
Avena sp. L. (awn)	oat awn	–	–	–	2	1	4	1	6
Avena L./*Bromus* L. sp.	oat/brome grass	6	52	32	40	36	45	59	97
Bromus sp. L.	brome grass	–	–	–	1	–	–	2	1
Monocot. Stem/rootlet frag		–	6	–	1	2	15	5	20
Bud		–	2	1	1	1	–	–	–
Parenchyma/Tuber		–	1	6	5	1	2	1	3
Triangular capsule frag		–	–	–	–	–	1	–	2

there is a higher percentage of chaff elements recorded in this sample than in the other assemblages. Other possible crops were again celtic bean, celtic bean/pea and oats. A few triangular capsules possibly of flax were also noted.

The weed seeds were dominated by seeds of vetch/weed pea which formed 38% of the assemblage. Other weed seeds included those of oat/brome grass, brassica, docks, cornflower, stinking mayweed, oxeye daisy and narrow-fruited cornsalad (*Valerianella dentata*), and runch capsules. These species are all typical of grassland, field margins and arable environments.

There were also hazelnut shell fragments, a sloe/hawthorn type thorn, monocotyledon stem fragments and grass culm nodes.

Discussion

The predominance of free-threshing wheat within the cereal remains, together with the presence of rye, barley and a few hulled wheat remains, in these assemblages is typical of assemblages of this date in Southern England (Greig 1991). The majority of the chaff elements of free-threshing wheat tend to be removed in the field by threshing and winnowing prior to storage. There is some spatial variation on the site with the grain-rich assemblages within the samples from the north and south ranges and pit 558 being indicative of the waste from stored grain, whereas those assemblages from enclosure system ditch 10034, pit 10025, posthole 534 and pit 633, where there was a higher percentage of weed seeds and/or chaff elements, may be more indicative of the waste from an earlier stage of processing, prior to storage. Other possible crops were celtic beans, peas, oats and flax. Free-threshing wheat, rye, barley, oats and flax were recorded from medieval deposits at Taunton Priory (Greig and Osborne 1984).

There is an indication from the weed seed assemblages of a number of different soil types being utilised for growing crops, with the use of sandier soils indicated by the presence of sheep's sorrel, of heavier clay soils shown by the occurrence of red bartsia and stinking mayweed, and of lighter drier calcareous soils favoured by weeds such as narrow-fruited cornsalad and small scabious. A similar range of species, reflecting a number of different soil types was also observed in assemblages from Taunton Priory (Greig and Osborne 1984).

Some of the species present, such as free-threshing wheat, rye, cornflower and stinking mayweed, are particularly indicative of Anglo-Saxon and medieval assemblages. It appears that stinking mayweed becomes more common in the Anglo-Saxon and medieval periods (Greig 1991) and is characteristic of the cultivation of heavy clay soils (Green 1984), associated with the change to mouldboard ploughs from ards (Jones 1981; Stevens with Robinson 2004; Stevens 2009) and the general increased cultivation of such heavier soils within the late Saxon period. It was noted in assemblages from medieval deposits at North Street, Stoke-sub-Hamdon (Ede 1992) and Taunton Priory (Greig and Osborne 1984).

The occasional possible exploitation of a hedgerow/scrub environment is indicated by the presence of hazelnut shell and sloe/hawthorn type thorns.

These assemblages appear to be more compatible generally with assemblages from rural medieval deposits, rather than those from high status sites, and there is no evidence for any large-scale crop production or processing on the site.

Chapter 7
Discussion

Prehistoric and Romano-British

The site at Longforth Farm is extensive, but there is relatively little that can be said about the early use of the area compared with what happened later during the medieval period. Nevertheless, there are several points of interest, particularly given that our knowledge of Wellington and its immediate surroundings in the prehistoric and Romano-British periods is very limited. This is not likely to reflect a genuine absence of evidence, rather a paucity of investigations.

A few early finds, mainly worked flint or chert, have been recorded in the area previously, and to this can be added a small number of Mesolithic, a single Neolithic and several possible Bronze Age pieces, the majority as residual finds from in or around channel 10002 in Area A. The single Terminal Upper Palaeolithic blade from the subsoil is a particularly noteworthy discovery and currently stands in isolation in the region.

Cropmark evidence has revealed a trapezoidal enclosure (HER 44166) approximately 1.5 km to the west of the site and a rectangular double-ditched enclosure (HER 44167) only 0.5 km to the north-west (see Fig. 1.1), but both are undated and could be either prehistoric or Romano-British, or possibly even later. The discovery, therefore, of the large part of a Middle Bronze Age Trevisker Ware vessel in the terminal of gully 10017 in Area B is significant, hinting at Bronze Age activity, conceivably of a ritual nature, in the vicinity of palaeochannel 10112. This gully also contained a notable deposit of burnt stone, perhaps the remains of a burnt mound associated with boiling water either for cooking or a prehistoric sauna. Other, possibly contemporary gullies suggest that there may have been some more formal land division of the area at this time. More convincing evidence for such a pattern comes from the later, albeit poorly dated features in Area A, for which a Late Bronze Age–Early Iron Age range has been tentatively suggested. Here, a complex of shallow ditches has been interpreted as forming part of a possible enclosure, perhaps double-ditched, with an adjacent field system. The lack of finds points towards this complex having served an agricultural purpose, with perhaps no contemporary settlement in the immediate vicinity.

Remains of Late Iron Age and Romano-British activity were sparse in the extreme, just a handful of sherds of pottery, and there have been few features or finds from the surrounding area. Quite extensive evaluations at Cade's Farm, which extended almost up to the south-east boundary of the site, produced very little, with no convincing evidence for Iron Age settlement and only two ditches and a cremation burial of probable Romano-British date. An initial evaluation (Oxford Archaeological Unit 1997) suggested the possibility of Roman pottery production, but no further evidence for this came from a second phase of trenching (Cotswold Archaeology 2005).

Medieval and Later

No Anglo-Saxon finds are recorded from Wellington, but the first documentary reference is in the early 10th century when a charter records it as part of an endowment of the new Bishopric of Wells. The estate was granted out of royal lands and a church, if not already present, is likely to have been established soon after, perhaps adjacent to a royal vill (Gathercole 2003). By the time of the *Domesday* survey in 1086 the population of *Walintone* had increased, and just over a century later, in 1215, Wellington received a royal grant according it borough status. It lay on the route between Bristol and Exeter and its commercial development, based on it being a market for the surrounding area, a place where fairs were held and later a local centre for cloth production can be largely attributed to the influence of the Bishops of Bath and Wells who held Wellington manor. The change to borough status also saw the layout of the town re-organised, with the church at the east end of what is now the High Street rather than at the centre of what remained a settlement of modest size and prosperity. The church, initially St Mary the Virgin, perhaps on the site of an Anglo-Saxon foundation, was largely rebuilt in the 15th century as St John the Baptist. It appears to have been a well-endowed foundation, though successive vicars chose to live at the linked centre of West Buckland rather than in Wellington itself. The rebuilt church has an impressively tall nave, with several 13th- or 14th-century elements of its predecessor surviving. One change before 1234

Plate 7.1 Overview of excavations in progress, with ancillary building in foreground, detached kitchen (centre right), and solar (left), hall (centre) and service range (right) beyond, from south-east

that might have had a bearing on medieval developments at Longforth Farm is the separation of the church and a small part of the estate to go towards the endowment of the new office of Provost of Wells.

Prior to 2011 nothing was known either from archaeological or documentary sources about any medieval settlement in the vicinity of Longforth Farm. However, the three 12th–14th-century pits recorded in the evaluation provided an indication of some activity, though there was nothing that foreshadowed the nature and status of the building complex that was subsequently uncovered (Pl. 7.1). This complex, approximately 1 km to the north of the church and the main route through medieval Wellington, seems most probably to date from the early 13th century. It could possibly be a few decades earlier, perhaps late 12th century, and conceivably had even earlier origins, but there is no convincing evidence for this. The earliest pottery amongst the relatively small assemblage probably belongs to the late 12th–13th century, and there is nothing to suggest that there was a preceding timber phase to the stone buildings.

Apart from the lack of close dating, the failure to locate any documentary records which relate specifically to the complex means that we do not know, in particular, who it was built for and belonged to and, therefore, what its precise function was.

The reason for choosing the site for the buildings is not immediately apparent. It lay a short distance from Wellington itself and was relatively low lying, with water management a probable issue, though built a little above the floodplain of the River Tone to the north. The evidence suggests that the palaeochannel immediately to the south was active at this time, as the peaty fill contained a very small amount of medieval material. Unfortunately, environmental sampling provided no useful information that might contribute to a better understanding of the contemporary local landscape. The palaeochannel may have been part of a small stream that flowed (until recently) from south-west to north-east along the north side of Area A (see Fig. 1.1), perhaps originally feeding into a pond, later known as Hobby Pond, to the west of Area B and the building complex. It is possible that Hobby Pond originated as a medieval fishpond associated with the building complex, and from this water then flowed north in an existing stream to join the original course of the River Tone approximately 300 m to the north.

Figure 7.1 Visualisation of north elevation of manor house, service range, detached kitchen and east end of ancillary building, from north-east

The topography of this area has been somewhat disrupted subsequently by 18th- and early 19th-century landscaping which included the diversion of this part of the Tone around the north side of Nynehead Park, the digging of a canal to the south (opened in 1835), and then by the construction of the Bristol and Exeter railway which came into use in 1843.

Another factor in the location of the building complex is that the site may not have been quite as isolated as it now appears, as a former route, known later as Old Lane, ran north-westwards from the east side of the church in Wellington to Nynehead (see Fig. 2.1). In doing so it passed immediately east of the medieval building complex and would have provided the principal means of access. To the north, Nynehead Court (Grade II*), extensively rebuilt in the late 17th and 18th centuries, contains elements of late 14th-century stonework (Historic England, List entry no. 1307540), a probable survival of the late medieval (and probably earlier) manor house there.

As indicated above, the evidence suggests that the construction of the complex at Longforth Farm most likely took place early in the 13th century, with no indication of a precursor or indeed any significant earlier medieval activity at the site. Ditch 10055 (see below) was the only feature containing medieval pottery that seems fairly certain to have predated the building complex, the small assemblage from this assigned a broad 11th–13th-century date. Furthermore, there is only limited evidence for any construction sequence or alterations amongst the various building remains. It appears from the plan at least to largely represent a single main phase of construction, though a range of rooms was added later, probably in the 14th century, to the east end of the core structure. There is also slight, though not very convincing evidence from the presence of a single ditch (10055) to suggest that the solar block was built after the hall and this might also explain the misalignment in the north wall between the two blocks. In general, however, the extensive and comprehensive robbing of stone from the complex means that any other relationships that might have been present have been obscured or destroyed, as has any clear evidence for the location of doorways.

Despite the ravages of stone robbing, the complex has been interpreted as a manor house largely on the basis of its plan form (Figs 3.4–5 and 7.1). Aspects of the various elements are considered in terms of their layout and likely function in comparison to other, better preserved or better understood examples (see, particularly, Wood 1965; Penoyre 2005; Barnwell and Adams 1994). The basic layout of medieval manor houses, or buildings of similar status, was fairly standard, with certain rooms or structures present, and usually arranged in a similar fashion.

The foundations of the buildings appeared to consist largely of chert, before giving way to shillet walling, a very small amount of which survived above ground level. There is no clear evidence for external rendering of what would have been a very rough surface to these stone walls. Door and window mouldings in a different, more easily carved stone, of which no fragments were recovered, are likely to have been of round-headed or two-centred form, with wooden shutters (no window glass was found), and the roof (of the main building at least) was covered in stone slates with glazed ceramic ridge tiles (Pl. 7.2). The overall effect would have been both impressive and striking within the immediately surrounding landscape.

The hall (Room 3 on Figs 3.4–5) was the principal room, as well as being the largest, and formed the focus of the complex. The visualisation offered here places it on the first floor (Fig. 7.2), which is primarily a 12th-century arrangement, but first floor halls were still being built in the 13th century, when ground floor halls became dominant, and certainly so in timber rather than stone buildings. The evidence here is equivocal, and from what remains it cannot be demonstrated with certainty that the hall at Longforth was at first floor level. This arrangement was originally primarily for defence, but became less of a necessity in the 13th century, when the ground floor space could then be used for storage, for example, and perhaps also for accommodation for retainers. A reference of 1383 to 'taking lime from the lord's cellar under the lord's hall' (see Chapter 2) may, therefore, be significant in this respect. Examples of surviving first floor halls include Saltford Manor near Bath (mid-12th century) (Penoyre 2005, 91–3), Boothby Pagnell, Lincolnshire (*c.* 1200) (Wood 1965, 19–21), Temple Manor, Strood, Kent (mid-13th century) (Rigold 1962) and Meare Manor House, Somerset (early 14th century) (Penoyre 2005, 103–5; Wood 1965, pl. Va). The nature of the timber roof structure at Longforth Farm is entirely speculative, but either arch braces below the collars of the main trusses, or scissor-braces, collars and rafters can be suggested as possibilities.

A courtyard or service yard, probably open to the west, lay to the south of the hall and it is assumed, therefore, that the principal entrance to the hall was on the north side. Here there appears to have been a walled forecourt, presumably with a gateway on the west or north side providing access to the lane between Wellington and Nynehead. The nature of the first floor entrance is uncertain, but on the basis of some admittedly slight remains it has been shown as a flight of steps at right angles to the hall (Fig. 7.1). Such an arrangement is unusual, but not unknown, for example the existing stairs at Boothby Pagnell (Wood 1965, fig. 6, pl. IVa) and also at Abingdon Checker, Oxfordshire (Wood 1965, 330), though more commonly the stairs were parallel to the building, as at Meare Manor House (Penoyre 2005, fig. 5.9) and Aydon Castle, Northumberland (Wood 1965, fig. 106). Stone steps are shown in the visualisation, but a combination of stone and timber is likely, and there may have been a timber porch.

The principal entrance would thus have lain towards the end of the hall nearest the service rooms,

Plate 7.2 Crested, glazed ridge tiles

as is normal, and away from the high end, which is likely to have been close to the solar or great chamber, the location of which can be confidently placed at the west end (see below). No evidence survived for any hearth or fireplace at ground floor level within the hall block, and the arrangements at first floor level must remain conjectural. However, a wall fireplace on the south side, on the opposite wall to the entrance, is suggested, as at Boothby Pagnell (Wood 1965, fig. 6), with a hood of wood and plaster supported on stone jambs, and a plain circular stone chimney of the type which appeared in the mid-12th century. Such a

Figure 7.2 Visualisation of interior of hall at first floor level

Plate 7.3 Decorated floor tiles

chimney, as present at Boothby Pagnell and 79½ High Street, Southampton (both *c.* 1200) (Wood 1965, 282, pls IVb and XLIVa), could have been supported by a shallow, flat buttress on the outside, though this may not have extended to ground level. However, an external buttress was found in this position on the south wall, and two others opposite this and further to the west on the north wall. Braziers could have been used to provide heat in the hall, and perhaps also in the solar.

The solar invariably lay beyond the upper end of the hall, at first floor level, and provided private accommodation for the family. The presence of a garderobe and the discovery of a number of glazed floor tiles to the west of the hall clearly indicate the location of the solar at Longforth Farm, as well as reflecting the status of the building (Pl. 7.3). This element comprised two or possibly three rooms, perhaps with storage space below. Immediately west of the hall was a relatively large, square room which is likely to have been the great chamber (Room 2), and beyond this the smaller private chamber or bedchamber (Room 1), with an integral garderobe or privy at the west end. This is similar to the late 13th-century arrangement at Old Soar, Plaxtol, Kent (Barnwell and Adams 1994, 10–11). The size and construction of the ground floor block of the garderobe shows a relatively sophisticated arrangement, designed to be periodically flushed by rainwater via a series of drains, though it would also have required regular cleaning out. At Bull Hill, a house possibly connected with nearby Pilton Priory (Devon), a box drain carried water which flushed the base of the garderobe (Wood 1965, 387). Part of Room 8 to the south of Room 1 may have served as a small private chapel, and the remainder of this narrow space, incorporated within rather than added to the building, may have accommodated a flight of stairs providing external access to the great chamber from the courtyard. This internal arrangement would be unusual, and more commonly external access to the solar was provided by a covered flight of steps on the outside wall, as at the Old Deanery, Salisbury (mid-13th century) (Wood 1965, 131 and 330). Chapels, where present, were often only accessible through the private rooms, some perhaps only separated from them by a timber partition. Such arrangements are found at Old Soar Manor, for example, the chapel here in a projecting block at the north-east corner of the solar (matching the latrine block at the north-west corner) (Barnwell and Adams 1994, 10–12), and at Charney Bassett manor house, Berkshire, also of late 13th-century date, where it adjoins the solar (Wood 1965, 230–1, fig. 69). The chapel floor is likely to have been paved, though the decorated floor tiles found in this area might equally come from either of the chambers. A similar discovery of decorated floor

Figure 7.3 Visualisation of courtyard and surrounding buildings, from south-west

tiles at West Thurrock manor house (Andrews 2009) was also used to suggest paving in the solar block there. The tiles at Longforth Farm indicate a mid–late 13th century date for the flooring (as at West Thurrock), possibly with more than one period of tile use, though the rooms themselves may be earlier and not initially tiled. As elsewhere at this level, timber planking would have been used, supported on heavy beams, with perhaps beaten earth on the ground floor.

At the opposite, lower end of the hall to the solar was the service range, and here there is evidence for two phases of construction, though there is no close dating for this sequence. The location of the service rooms is one found in many excavated as well as extant manorial complexes of the 13th and 14th centuries, whether they had ground floor, open or first floor halls, for example Copton Manor, Sheldwich and Igtham Moat, both in Kent and dating to *c.* 1330 (Barnwell and Adams 1994, 10–11). At Longforth Farm, Rooms 4 and 5 immediately east of the hall were the earliest and appear contemporary with it. Room 4, the larger of the two, was most likely the buttery, used for the storage of food and drink, with Room 5, the narrow space to the south, perhaps housing an internal flight of stairs from the ground floor. An alternative possibility is that the buttery was on the ground floor and there was a guest chamber above this. Rooms 6 and 7 beyond had been added later, and effectively formed a cross wing (Fig. 7.1), with the remains of a possible central hearth in Room 6 suggesting that this space could have been a kitchen and, therefore, open to the roof. The attaching of the kitchen to the main house, however, appears to be a later 15th century development and, therefore, somewhat later than is suggested for the demise of the complex here. Perhaps the additional space provided by Rooms 6 and 7 was used for service purposes or the storage of other materials. Conceivably, though perhaps less likely, it provided accommodation for guests and visitors. It may be from the service end of the main house that the plain floor tiles derive, some worn smooth through use.

Prior to the late 15th century, in manorial and other high status complexes, as well as more humble dwellings, the preparation and cooking of food is likely to have taken place in a detached kitchen, thereby reducing the risk of fire spreading to the rest of the house should things get out of control. Such kitchens would have had a central hearth for roasting, and perhaps one or two smaller ovens for baking, all set within what was often a timber-framed, plastered structure open to the eaves. Their relatively insubstantial foundations are likely to account for the paucity of surviving evidence here, and the suggested location close to the service range is entirely appropriate. It is one seen elsewhere, for example at Randall Manor, Shorne, Kent (Mayfield 2014), and Northolt Manor, Middlesex (Wood 1965, 248) (both of 13th century date), sometimes with a pentice providing a covered link between them. The apparent alignment between the site of the detached kitchen (Room 9) and Rooms 6 and 7 to the north, with a narrow gap or passageway between them, is of interest, as it suggests that they were contemporary. Perhaps Rooms 6 and 7 were originally built largely in timber and later replaced in stone, or perhaps the location of the detached kitchen represents its final position after one or more rebuilds, a common occurrence amongst such structures that were occasionally burnt down.

The detached kitchen lay on the east side of the small courtyard or service court to the rear of the hall, with a relatively long, narrow building (Room 10) along the south side (Fig. 7.3). The function of this ancillary building is not known, but the buttresses at the east end indicate a possible two-storey structure, perhaps of stone here with the remainder wholly or partly of timber at first floor level. The drain running through the east end of the building and apparently feeding water into the courtyard from the palaeochannel, rather than vice versa, may be unrelated to its function, and it may have served as a store, stables or perhaps guest accommodation (at least at first floor level), or a combination of such purposes. The western end of the ancillary building did not survive, nor any structures beyond this, such as a brewhouse which perhaps might be expected, in addition to stables. It is possible that some of these buildings were thatched rather than tiled. Similar structures have been found during recent excavations at Randall Manor, Shorne, including at least two relatively long, narrow buildings on two sides of the service court, which also contained a detached kitchen and a brewhouse (Mayfield 2014).

At Longforth Farm, other ancillary structures may have lain around the edge of the walled forecourt to the north, the extent of which is unknown, but it is equally likely that this was kept largely or completely clear of buildings as it formed the principal approach and entrance to the complex.

The ditches to the east of the building complex, away from the main access, reflect an associated system of enclosures, some possibly paddocks. However, the enclosure immediately to the east appears to have had direct access from the courtyard and perhaps functioned as an adjunct to the service range and detached kitchen, and may have been an open-air area where related activities were undertaken. This western enclosure and the relatively small number of associated pits have been dated to the 14th century, the likely date of the extension of the service range, with their use probably continuing into the earlier part of the 15th century. The easternmost enclosure contained the remnants of a possibly circular structure, conceivably a pig sty. A cluster of pits in this area may have been for quarrying clay, but these and the few other pits, as well as the enclosure ditches, produced relatively few finds. However, the pottery from these enclosure ditches is earlier than that from the western ditches, with a broad date range spanning the 11th–13th centuries, with a likely focus in the latter century, and all are likely to have been associated with the building complex rather than predating it.

The limited environmental evidence, with threshing waste from the enclosure ditches and charred plant remains indicative of processed grain from the service range, tells us a little about the economy of the complex, though the nature and distribution of this material is not unexpected. The faunal assemblage is small, but there is certain to have been a combination of arable agriculture and animal husbandry, probably with fish obtained from the nearby pond. Unfortunately, it is the nature of many such high status sites that they were kept relatively clean, with domestic debris disposed of on middens, of which no trace has survived, or directly on to fields, and the few pits produced very little. One can note, however, the unusual occurrence (in Somerset) of two costrels (see Mepham, Chapter 5, Pl. 5.1), an uncommon type of ceramic container, and the one – possibly two sherds of Saintonge polychrome pottery, rarely found on sites away from the major south coast ports. This paucity of finds was also the case, for example, at the medieval manor house at West Thurrock (Andrews 2009). There is, therefore, very little amongst the animal bone, charred plant remains and pottery that can provide more detailed information on the agricultural economy and status of the site.

This is also true also for the restricted number and range of other finds, and it is only the glazed crested ridge tiles and, in particular, the decorated floor tiles that indicate, in conjunction with the layout and construction of the complex, that something rather more than a medieval farmstead is represented (see Mepham, Chapter 4; Pls 7.2–3).

Ascertaining when the use of the complex at Longforth Farm ceased is even more difficult than ascribing a date to the beginning, but its decline seems to have been rapid, with no indication of a prolonged period of decay and gradual abandonment. At some time in the late 14th or the early 15th century is considered most likely, though on little secure evidence, this dating relying almost entirely on the somewhat scant late medieval and early post-medieval pottery assemblage. Certainly, the buildings were comprehensively robbed, presumably to recover virtually all reusable stone including door and window mouldings, general walling material and roof tiles.

If the door and window mouldings were set into ashlar stone facings, then some damage might be expected to have occurred to them during removal, leading to fragments becoming part of the site debris. If the walling was largely shillet, however, as seems likely, then it may have afforded relatively easy

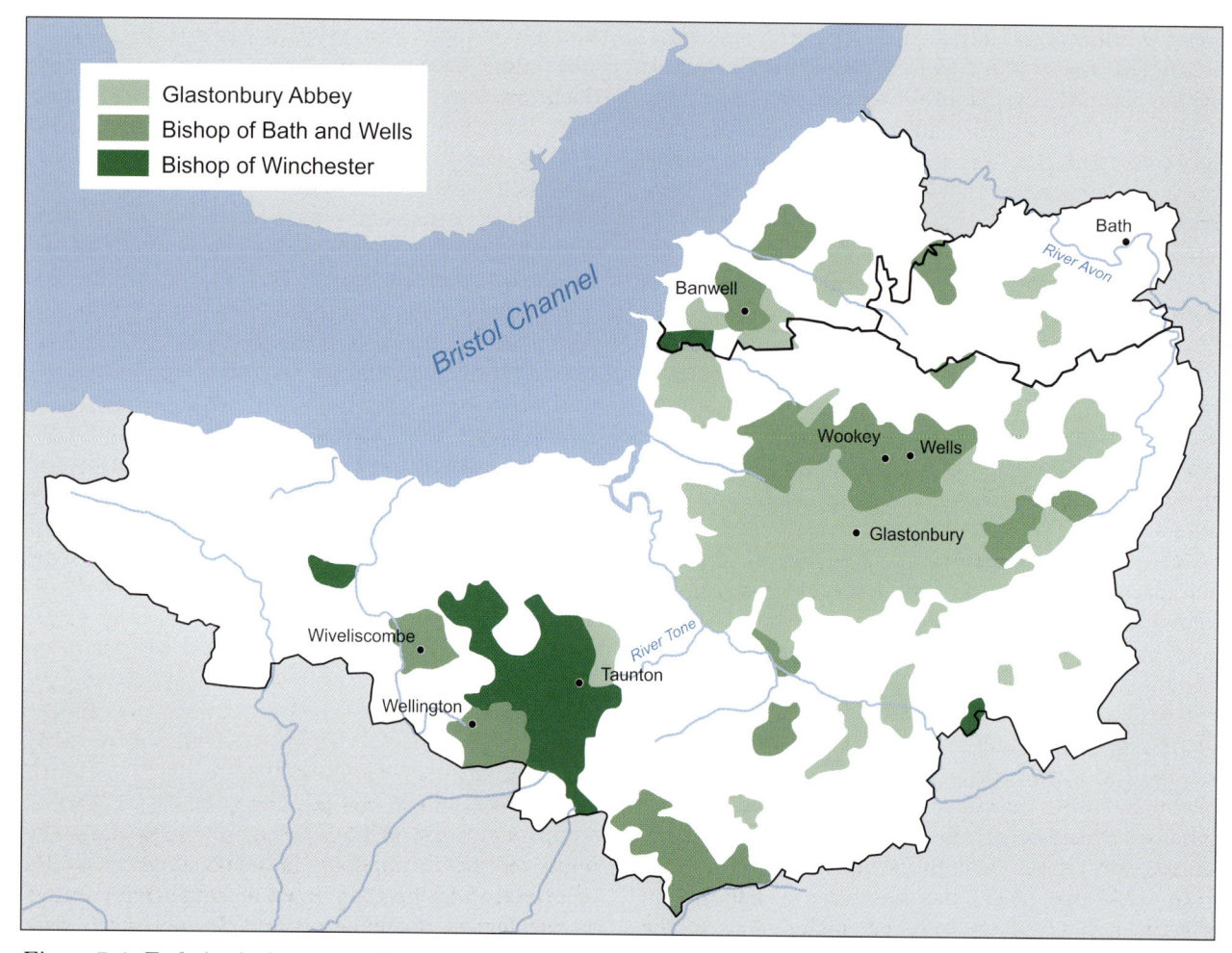

Figure 7.4 Ecclesiastical estates in Somerset (after Aston 1988)

extraction of the moulded frames. A building of the size and quality that appears to be the case here would have had a number of such mouldings, standing out from the plainer wall fabric. This walling material was also extensively removed, leaving mainly wall foundations of smaller, tightly packed chert behind. The relatively large number of roof slate fragments is easier to explain, as when stripped from the roof, the retaining wooden pegs or iron nails may have been difficult to remove, breaking some of the slates in the process, which were then discarded. The one anomaly in this process of stone robbing is the base of the garderobe, which was largely left untouched, perhaps avoided because of its former use?

The few poorly dated post-medieval spreads and the two pairs of ditches crossing the site of the former complex are thought most likely to relate to the phase of robbing, as it is difficult to explain their presence and arrangement otherwise. The stone recovered may have gone for reuse in various buildings in and around Wellington, but perhaps much of it went to a single site, the possible implications of which are considered further below.

The robbing of the complex marked the end of the building sequence on the site, which then reverted to agricultural use, with apparently no historical, field name or other evidence surviving to reflect the former presence of such a high status complex. A small hint might, however, be provided by the field name of Culverhayes, which lay to the north, signifying the presence of a dovecot. Could this field name, of 18th century or earlier date, indicate the former presence of a structure some three centuries earlier and possibly associated with the complex in question?

Conclusion

In the absence of any explicit documentary evidence, all strands of information need to be considered together to tease out a little more about the history of the medieval building complex at Longforth Farm. It does seem clear that it was in existence throughout most of the 13th and 14th centuries, perhaps a little earlier and probably a little later.

The Bishops of Bath and Wells held the manor, and the award of borough status to Wellington in 1215 may have been the catalyst which led to the construction of the building complex at Longforth Farm, during the two decades that the bishops' seat was at Glastonbury. The seat of the Bishops of Bath and Wells was established at Wells in 1245, though prior to this it had moved on several occasions. Initially at Wells in *c.* 909, the seat transferred to Bath in 1090, was at Glastonbury for a short period between 1197 and 1219, and then Bath again from 1219 to 1245, before its final move to Wells where it has remained for almost 800 years.

It is suggested here that the building complex at Longforth Farm was the medieval manor house of the bishops, where they held their court, the location of which is unknown. Though not close to the church, as might be expected, the newly discovered complex would have been less than 1 km away on a well-established route to Nynehead, and in its layout, size and status is undoubtedly what can be classed as a manor house.

The bishops rarely visited Wellington, Wiveliscombe just 8 km to the north-west being preferred, at least in the 14th century, and they also had retreats on other ecclesiastical estates, the best known being at Wookey and Banwell (Fig. 7.4). Perhaps they also had one on their estate at Wellington which they used as an occasional retreat mainly during the 13th century. The possibility that Sir John de Molton may have been the tenant of the bishops' manor house in 1343 has been mentioned above, though the location is not given. Also, it is from 1343 to 1383 that we have a handful of references in the court rolls that include two to the houses in the Court at Wellington requiring repair and thatching, perhaps by then a century and a half old, and another concerning taking lime from the lord's cellar under the lord's hall. Might this indicate a hall at first floor level as has been suggested for the main building here?

The decorated floor tiles also offer further clues, but we cannot be sure of their precise significance. Nevertheless, as has been pointed out above, the parallels in Somerset are all with ecclesiastical sites, in particular Glastonbury Abbey but also Wells Cathedral. The heraldic tiles (Fig. 4.3, 6, Pl. 7.3) may offer a link to the St Barbe family, first recorded *c.* 1210, who probably came over at the Conquest and later held land in Somerset, or possibly the de Warenne's; it was William de Warenne, 5th Earl of Surrey (tenure 1202–1240), who established Salisbury Cathedral.

The documents are silent after 1383, and there is no indication that the bishops visited in the 15th century, maybe leading to the demise of their manor house. Perhaps it is also relevant to note that when the Popham's built their new court house within the town in the early 17th century (see Fig. 1.1), it may have been on or near to the site of what was said to be a 15th-century Borough court house, the latter conceivably a successor to the bishops' medieval manor house. This Borough court house, most likely located close to the High Street, may have been the destination of much of the stone robbed from the now redundant and abandoned Longforth Farm complex, though possibly some material found its way into the church of St John the Baptist, built on the site of St Mary's in the early 15th century

The conclusion reached here, that the building complex at Longforth Farm was the medieval manor house of the Bishops of Bath and Wells, may be incorrect, and is perhaps based on somewhat tenuous archaeological, documentary and chronological links. Nevertheless, it was clearly a substantial, high status building which appears to have completely disappeared from the historical records. The possibility remains, however, that one day in the future such records might be discovered, perhaps in an ecclesiastic archive somewhere, during the course of some unrelated research, which will confirm its owners and tenants, when it was built and the date and reason for its demise.

Bibliography

Allan, J P, 1984 *Medieval and Post-Medieval Finds from Exeter, 1971–1980*, Exeter Archaeol Rep 3

Allan, J P, 2003 A group of early 13th-century pottery from Sherborne Old Castle and its wider context, *Proc Dorset Natur Hist Archaeol Soc* 125, 71–82

Allan, J P, Hughes, M J and Taylor, R T, 2010 Saxo-Norman pottery in Somerset: some recent research, *Proc Somerset Archaeol Natur Hist Soc* 154, 165–84

Andrews, P, 2009 West Thurrock: Late prehistoric settlement, Roman burials and the medieval manor house, Channel Tunnel Rail Link Excavations 2002, *Essex Archaeol and Hist* 40, 1–77

Aston, M, 1988 *Aspects of the Medieval Landscape of Somerset*, Taunton, Somerset County Council

Barnwell, P S and Adams, A T, 1994 *The House Within: interpreting medieval houses in Kent*, London, HMSO

British Geological Survey (BGS), 2013, http://mapapps.bgs.ac.uk/geologyofbritain/home.html (accessed 28 November 2013)

Bournemouth University, 2010 *Longforth Farm, Wellington, Somerset, Geophysical Survey Interim Report*, Bournemouth, unpubl rep

Coleman-Smith, R and Pearson, T, 1988, *Excavations in the Donyatt Potteries*, Chichester, Phillimore

Cotswold Archaeology, 2005 *Cade's Farm, Wellington, Somerset: Archaeological Evaluation*, Cirencester, unpubl rep

Cotswold Archaeology, 2011a *Land at Longforth Farm, Wellington, Somerset: Archaeological Evaluation*, Cirencester, unpubl rep

Cotswold Archaeology, 2011b *Land at Longforth Farm, Wellington, Somerset: Written Scheme of Investigation for an Archaeological Strip, Map and Record Exercise*, Cirencester, unpubl rep

Croft, R A, 1987 Wellington, St John's Church, *Proc Somerset Archaeol Natur Hist Soc* 127, 29

Drury, P, 2001 Discussion of the Wells tiles, their affinities and dating, in Rodwell 2001, 455–9

Dunning, G C, 1964 Barrel-shaped and cylindrical costrels on the Continent and in England, in B Cunliffe *Winchester Excavations 1949–1960, Vol. 1*, Winchester, 127–40

Eames, E, 1988 The tile kiln and floor tiles, in T B James and A M Robinson, *Clarendon Palace: the history and archaeology of a medieval palace and hunting lodge near Salisbury, Wiltshire*, Rep Res Comm Soc Antiq London 45, 127–67

Ede, J, 1992 Carbonised plant material, in R Montague, C M Hearne and D E Farwell Excavations at North Street, Stoke sub Hamdon, 1992, *Proc Somerset Archaeol Natur Hist Soc* 136 [1993], 103–15

Gathercole, C, 2003 *An Archaeological Assessment of Wellington*, English Heritage Extensive Urban Survey/Somerset County Council

Green, F J, 1984 The archaeological and documentary evidence for plants from the Medieval period in England, in W van Zeist and W A Casparie (eds) *Plants and Ancient Man: studies in palaeoethnobotany*, Proceedings of the 6th Symposium of the IWGP. Rotterdam, Balkema, 99–144

Greig J, 1991 The British Isles, in W van Zeist, K Wasylikowa and K-E Behre (eds) *Progress in Old World Palaeoethnobotany*, Rotterdam, 229–334

Greig, J R A and Osborne P J, 1984 Plant and insect remains at Taunton Priory, in P Leach (ed.) *The Archaeology of Taunton: excavations and fieldwork to 1980*, Bristol, Western Archaeological Trust Excavation Monogr 8, 160–5

Harcourt, J, 2000 The medieval floor-tiles of Cleeve Abbey, Somerset, *J Brit Archaeol Assoc* 153, 30–70

Hare, J N, 1991 The growth of the roof-tile industry in later medieval Wessex, *Medieval Archaeol* 35, 86–103

Holbrook, N and Bidwell, P, 1991 *Roman Finds from Exeter*, Exeter, Exeter Archaeol Rep 4

Humphreys, A L, 1910 *Materials for the History and Parish of Wellington, Part II: Manorial Court Rolls*, 172, 174, 180, 182–3

Hurst, J G, Neal, D S and van Beuningen, H J E, 1986 *Pottery Produced and Traded in North-West Europe 1350–1650*, Rotterdam, Rotterdam Papers VI

Jones, M K, 1981 The development of crop husbandry, in M K Jones and G Dimbleby (eds) *The Environment of Man, the Iron Age to the Anglo-Saxon Period*, Oxford, BAR 87, 95–127

Le Patourel, H E J, 1968 Documentary evidence and the medieval pottery industry, *Medieval Archaeol* 12, 101–26

Mayfield, A, 2014 Community Archaeology Excavations at Randall Manor, Kent, *Rosetta* 15, 87–8

Lowe, B, 2003 *Decorated Medieval Floor Tiles of Somerset. Taunton, Somerset*, Archaeol Natur Hist Soc and Somerset County Museums Service

Medieval Pottery Research Group (MPRG) 1998 *A Guide to the Classification of Medieval Ceramic Forms*, Medieval Pottery Res Group Occas Paper 1

Medieval Pottery Research Group (MPRG) 2001 *Minimum Standards for the Processing, Recording, Analysis and Publication of Post-Roman Ceramics*, Medieval Pottery Res Group Occas Paper 2

Morris, E L, 1994 *The Analysis of Pottery*, Salisbury, Wessex Archaeology Guideline 4

Oxford Archaeological Unit (OAU) 1997 *Cade's Farm, Taunton Road, Wellington, Somerset: Archaeological Evaluation Report*, unpubl rep

Parker Pearson, M, 1990 The production and distribution of Bronze Age pottery in south-west Britain, *Cornish Archaeol* 29, 5–32

Parker Pearson, M, 1995 Southwestern Bronze Age pottery, in I Kinnes and G Varndell (eds) *'Unbaked Urns of Rudely shape': essays on British and Irish pottery for Ian Longworth*, Oxford, Oxbow Monogr 55, 89–100

Pearson, T, 1984 Medieval and post-medieval ceramics in Taunton, in P Leach *The Archaeology of Taunton*, Western Archaeol Trust Excav Monogr 8, 142–44; microfiche 1–2

Penoyre, J, 2005 *Traditional Houses of Somerset*, Tiverton, Somerset Books

Prehistoric Ceramic Research Group (PCRG), 2010 *The Study of Later Prehistoric Pottery: general policies and guidelines for analysis and publication*, Prehistoric Ceramics Res Group Occasional Paper 1/2 (3rd edition)

Quinnell H, 2012, Trevisker pottery: some recent studies, in W J Britnell and R J Silvester (eds) *Reflections on the Past: essays in honour of Frances Lynch*, Welshpool, Cambrian Archaeological Association, 146–71

Rigold, S E, 1962 *Temple Manor, Strood, Rochester, Kent*, Ministry of Works

Rodwell, W, 2001 *Wells Cathedral: Excavations and Structural Studies, 1978–93*, English Heritage Archaeol Rep 21

Salzmann, L E, 1952 *Building in England Down to 1540: a documentary history*, Oxford, Clarendon Press

Stace, C, 1997 *New flora of the British Isles*. Cambridge, Cambridge Univ Press (2nd edition)

Stevens, C J, 2009 Charred plant remains, in P Andrews, K Egging Dinwiddy, C Ellis, A Hutcheson, C Phillpotts, A Powell, and J Schuster *Kentish Sites and Sites of Kent. A miscellany of four archaeological excavations*, Salisbury, Wessex Archaeology Report 24, 41–7

Stevens, C J with Robinson, M, 2004 Production and consumption: plant cultivation, in G Hey *Yarnton: Saxon and Medieval Settlement and Landscape*, Thames Valley Landscape Monograph 20, Oxford, Oxford Archaeological Unit, 81–2

Terence O'Rourke Ltd, 2011 *Longforth Farm, Wellington, Somerset: Desk-based archaeology assessment*, unpubl rep

Thorp, J, 1996 The excavated slates and slate hanging, in S Brown, Berry Pomeroy Castle, *Proc Devon Archaeol Soc* 54, 291–4

Timby, J, 1989 The Roman Pottery, in P Ellis, Norton Fitzwarren hillfort: a report on the excavations by Nancy and Phillip Langmaid between 1968 and 1971, *Proc Somerset Archaeol Natur Hist Soc* 133, 53–9

Wessex Archaeology, 2014 *A High Status Medieval Building Complex at Longforth Farm, Wellington, Somerset: post-excavation assessment and updated project design*, Salisbury, unpubl rep 85402.1

Wessex Archaeology, 2016 *Land at West Camel Road, Queen Camel, Somerset: post-excavation assessment and updated project design*, Salisbury, unpubl rep 102840.03

Wessex Archaeology and Jacobi, R, 2014 *Palaeolithic and Mesolithic Lithic Artefact (PaMELA) database*, http://archaeologydataservice.ac.uk/archives/view/pamela_2014/ (accessed 11 September 2015)

Wood, M, 1965 *The English Medieval House*, London, J M Dent & Sons Ltd

Woodward, A, 1989 Prehistoric pottery, in P Ellis, Norton Fitzwarren hillfort: a report on the excavations by Nancy and Phillip Langmaid between 1968 and 1971, *Proc Somerset Archaeol Natur Hist Soc* 133, 39–53

Zohary, D and Hopf, M, 2000 *Domestication of plants in the Old World: the origin and spread of cultivated plants in West Asia, Europe, and the Nile Valley*, Oxford, Clarendon Press (3rd edition)

Historical and documentary sources

Cornwall Record Office, AR/1/1101
Greenwood's map of Somerset 1822
History of the Walcott Family; SHC (Somerset Heritage Centre), DD/SF 2/5719
Register of Bishop Drokensford, Somerset Record Society vol. 1, pp. 8, 108 and 481
Register of Bishop Ralph of Shrewsbury, Somerset Record Society vol. 9, pp. xxxii–xxxvi
SHC (Somerset Heritage Centre), A/DAE 1/15
SHC (Somerset Heritage Centre), DD/DP 35/3, 42/5, 63/3, 64/3, 73/2, 85/5, 93/9
SHC (Somerset Heritage Centre) DD/SF 2/42/71
SHC (Somerset Heritage Centre), Q/REI 24/5
SHC (Somerset Heritage Centre), Wellington tithe award 1839